DATE DUE

FEB 2 2000	NOV 17 2014
FEB 2 6 2000	MAY 0 1 2015
MAR 2 3 2000	JUN 2 6 2021
MAY 0 5 2000	
JUN 0 8 2000	
JUN 2 1 2000	
FEB 1 4 2004	
JAN 2 6 2005	
MAR 2 7 2006	
OCT 2 7 2008	
DEC 1 2008	
JAN 1 2 2009	
NOV 1 3 2009	
MAR 2 8 2014	
AUG 3 1 2014	
OCT 2 4 2014	

BRODART, CO.

D1602950

STIRRUP HIGH

By Walt Coburn

DECORATIONS BY ROSS SANTEE

FOREWORD BY FRED GIPSON

Introduction to the Bison Books Edition by
Dale L. Walker

University of Nebraska Press
Lincoln

⊗ The paper in this book meets the minimum requirements of American National Standard for Information Sciences—Permanence of Paper for Printed Library Materials, ANSI Z39.48-1984.

First Bison Books printing: 1997
Most recent printing indicated by the last digit below:
10   9   8   7   6   5   4   3   2   1

Library of Congress Cataloging-in-Publication Data
Coburn, Walt, 1889–1971.
Stirrup high / by Walt Coburn; introduction by Dale L. Walker.
p.   cm.
ISBN 0-8032-6377-5 (pbk.: alk. paper)
1. Coburn, Walt, 1889–1971—Childhood and youth.   2. Novelists, American—20th century—Biography.   3. Montana—Social life and customs.   4. Teenage boys—Montana—Biography.   5. Ranch life—Montana.   6. Cowboys—Montana.   I. Title.
PS3505.0153Z464   1997
813′.52—dc21
[B]
96-47112   CIP

Reprinted from the original 1957 edition by Julian Messner, Inc., New York.

To the memory of my father
ROBERT COBURN
who braved the hardships and dangers
of a pioneer cattleman,
and to the old-time cowhands
who worked for the Circle C
when I was stirrup high

CONTENTS

INTRODUCTION

Dale L. Walker

When Walt Coburn died near Prescott, Arizona, on 24 May 1971, his long-time friend, the actor Walter Brennan, said, "I miss him not so much for the things he said, because I can read them in the thousand stories and books he wrote. I miss him for his keen mind and eye to what was truly Western."

That mind and eye was especially keen in Coburn's nonfiction work—in his *Pioneer Cattleman in Montana: The Story of the Circle C Ranch* (1968), and most notably in *Stirrup High* (1957), the most "truly Western" and charming of all his books, now revived from an undeserved obscurity by the University of Nebraska Press.

To appreciate the Westernness and charm of *Stirrup High*, it is helpful to know something about the author and how he came to tell this story of that summer of 1903 when he was fourteen and stirrup high to his cow pony Snowflake, and how he learned the cow business and earned his spurs.

Walter P. "Walt" Coburn, born in 1889 in White Sulphur Springs, Montana, grew up in Great Falls and on his family's thirty-thousand-acre Circle C ranch near the town of Zortman in the northeastern remoteness of Montana Territory, twenty miles north of the Missouri River and sixty miles from the Canadian border.

His father, a stern, fearless man with a strict code of conduct for himself, his family and his cowboys, had pioneered westward, following the gold rush to Virginia City in 1863. He had been among the vigilantes who hanged the renegade lawman Henry Plummer at Bannack in 1864, came to know Chief Joseph of the Nez Perce, and built one of the biggest cow outfits in the Territory.

Young Walt's mother and sisters—who avoided the rough life on the isolated ranch—lived in Great Falls, and there he attended high school, spending his summers—looking forward to every one of them—with his father on the Circle C. In his late teens, probably at his mother's insistence, he attended the Manzanita Preparatory School in Palo Alto, California, readying for entrance at Stanford University. But he did not complete the course of study and returned to Montana, where he worked as a hand on the Circle C until his father sold the ranch in 1916.

Coburn served as a sergeant in the Signal Corps, Air Corps branch, in World War One; worked on a cattle spread near Globe, Arizona, after the war; and after a bull-roping accident ended his cowboying days, began, in 1922, writing Western stories.

He got a late start as a writer but his timing was nearly perfect and he made up for lost time.

In July 1922, when he was thirty-three, Coburn's first story, "The Peace Treaty of the Seven-Up," appeared in *Argosy*, the respected Munsey magazine, among the first all-fiction periodicals in the United States and one which had published writers of the caliber of O. Henry, James Branch Cabell, Albert Payson Terhune, William McLeod Raine, and P. G. Wodehouse.

Then, four months after the *Argosy* debut, Coburn began a twenty-seven-year association with *Western Story Magazine*, the most durable of the Western "pulps" (so-called for their cheap, ragged-edged paper.) This magazine, which often ran 136 pages of fiction (usually a novel, two serials, and three short stories) plus a nonfiction piece, letters and miscellaneous "departments," was the first real all-Western pulp, having converted from the dime novel *Buffalo Bill Weekly* in 1919. In its three-decade history, *Western Story*, a weekly with a circulation at one time of 300,000, regularly published William Colt McDonald, Frederick D. Glidden ("Luke Short"), W. C. Tuttle, and, the King of the Pulps, Frederick Faust ("Max Brand"), among others considered the best Western writers of the era. Faust-as-Brand often contributed as many as three stories in one issue of *Western Story*. His nearest competitor in the 1930s was Walt Coburn who, from 1938 until the magazine's demise in 1949, wrote every cover story and often one or two additional ones per issue.

Besides *Western Story*, Coburn wrote regularly for such pulps as *Adventure, Action Stories, Cowboy Story, North-West Stories, Star Western, All Western, Romance, Complete Story*, and *West*, a Western fiction magazine published in England.

So prolific was his fiction production that two periodicals carried his name in their titles—*Walt Coburn's Action Novels* in the 1930s and *Walt Coburn's Western Magazine* published in 1949–50, at the end of the pulp era.

Coburn's first novel published in book form, *The Ringtailed Rannyhans*, appeared in 1927; his last, *Reckless*, in 1968. He produced thirty-four novels in hardcover and paperback for such houses as Century, Fiction House, Messner, Macfadden, Lippincott, Hammond (in England), Ace, Lancer, Avon, Berkley, and Belmont. Today few remember *Law Rides the Range, Pardners of the Dim Trails, Beyond the Wild Missouri, Wet Cattle, Gun Grudge, The Night Branders.*

In a writing career just shy of fifty years Coburn published an astonishing nine hundred stories in thirty-seven magazines, thirty-four novels, and an assortment of autobiographical works. He wrote a minimum of 2,000 publishable words a day, six days a week, his 600,000 word output the equivalent of seven or eight fair-sized books annually. If he was not King (a title bestowed on Frederick Faust) Coburn was at least a Prince of the Pulps and earned a good living from them for nearly thirty years.

Since Coburn's fiction owed more to the pulp formula than to the real West, Walter Brennan, when he spoke of his friend's "keen mind and eye to what was truly Western," may have had *Stirrup High* in mind. It is Coburn's best book and may be the single work that will preserve the author's name.

Stirrup High, which has been categorized as a "Western juvenile," actually appeals to the general reader and nostalgia buff as well as to the young adult reader, at whom Coburn probably aimed the story. Although autobiographical, like Andy Adams's *Log of a Cowboy* (1903), the book makes use of classic fictional techniques which, in Coburn's case, were employed in his trade as pulp fictioneer: lots of dialogue, plenty of action (a harness race, bronc-busting, swimming cattle across the Missouri River, stealing milk and butter from a sheepherder's camp), use of humor, and the tone and pace of a yarn spun around a campfire. Many of the archetypical characters were based on real Circle C cowmen (Horace Brewster, for example, the roundup boss from whom Coburn learned more of the cow business than from his own father). And young Coburn had met Harvey Logan, alias "Kid Curry" of the Wild Bunch, that summer on roundup.

The result is a splendid, authentic glimpse, funny and lovingly told, of a Montana summer in 1903 and a fourteen-year-old boy's adventures and education among cows and cowboys. Coburn expertly evokes the time through his recollections of seeing Dustin Farnum in the silent movie version of Owen Wister's *The Virginian* (and realizing that his *hero* from the story is the outlaw Trampas), through such events as sneaking a smoke of Bull Durham when out of sight of his father's ranch house, riding in a Concord stagecoach to the cowtown of Malta, exploring the mysteries and romance of the blacksmith's shop, and relishing such chuckwagon fare as Four X Arbuckles' coffee and sourdough biscuits soaked in chokecherry syrup.

In his fiction, Coburn, like virtually all his Western pulp-writing contemporaries, appealed to his editors and to their notions of what their readers wanted, by telling stories of an utterly mythic West. In *Stirrup High*, this "shy little sawed-off ex-Montana cowhand," as his Texas friend Fred Gipson (author of *Hound Dog Man* and *Old Yeller*), called him, told of a real West, one that he experienced as a youth and loved.

Reading the ebullient *Stirrup High* makes it clear that Coburn preferred the real one over the mythic.

A working writer quite often gets hazed into the so-called "literary circles" and endless discussions of what factors go into the make-up of good writing. He is bombarded with long-winded expositions on "story form," "writing style," and some highly technical but indefinable thing called "literary symbolism."

What he never hears discussed at such gatherings is which end of a cow gets up off the ground first.

This may not seem like a subject very closely related to the art of writing. Yet if you'll read a little way into one of Walt Coburn's yarns, you'll soon see the connection.

It's obvious from the start that this shy little sawed-off ex-Montana cowhand knows which end of a cow gets up first. He knows, too, which end of a horse gets up first—

and the color of burnt-hair smoke, curling up from under a hot branding iron—what raindrops smell like when they first start kicking up the dry prairie dust—what it's like to feel your saddle slipping beneath the belly of a fear-crazed horse—the terror of riding blind in a cattle stampede in the dead of night.

His ability to re-live his first-hand experience of cows and horses and men through his yarns is the quality that has made my friend Coburn one of the leading writers of the Old West for more years than he likes to remember.

In this latest tale of his, STIRRUP HIGH, the veteran word-wrangler reaches 'way back to his beginnings—back to a long-ago summer when he first tried to make a hand among the tough Montana riders who worked his father's Circle C range—back to the time when he began picking up this special knowledge of the range—back to a way of life that's gone forever.

And, as usual, it's jam-packed with his knowledge of range lore, so that from the start the reader finds himself right out in the middle of the story, knowing—or learning fast—the whys and wherefores of every piece of action that takes place.

STIRRUP HIGH may be short on "literary symbolism," but it has Walt's own natural story sense and his own realistic conversational style. It's the sort of action story I like to read—written by a man who knows which end of a cow gets up first.

Fred Gipson

Mason, Texas
June, 1957

Stirrup High

CHAPTER ONE

So Long School Days

For me the ninth of June, the last day of school, had a meaning far beyond the average schoolboy's dreams. It stretched to the far sky line of the unfenced range of my father's Circle C ranch at the foot of the Little Rockies in northeastern Montana.

I was fourteen and small for my age, about stirrup high to my cow pony Snowflake waiting at the ranch for me.

My saddle and Navajo saddle blanket and bridle had been in a canvas sack that had once held navy beans, for two weeks now, stored in the basement of our three-storied white house in Great Falls. My valise was packed with a dozen brand-new black sateen shirts, three pair of Levi's, a pair of buckskin gloves, underwear and socks. My new Stetson hat hung on the hatrack in the front hall, the crown carefully dented in four places.

I had a haircut the day before, and I was scrubbed and dressed in my Norfolk corduroy jacket and short pants, knee-length stockings, white shirt, and red Windsor tie. The train for Malta, where I would get off and take the stagecoach for the ranch, left at five o'clock in the afternoon. I was ready to go when Old Tom, our coachman, hitched up Big Ned, our carriage horse, and drove me to the station. I had two five-dollar bills and some change in

13

the pocket of my short pants, together with the family railway pass, issued to all cattlemen by the Great Northern Railway.

My mother and sisters fussed over me with their goodbys, and I was glad when Old Tom loaded my saddle and valise, and we drove off. I was gladder still when they didn't insist on seeing me off on the train.

This was the first time I was making the trip alone. Always before my father had come along and he'd made me send my sacked saddle in the express car. But this time I was handling it myself, like I'd seen the cowpunchers do when they traveled by train. I wanted everybody to know what was in the sack, so I let the horn stick out.

I had my hat on at a jack-deuce slant and wished I had on the rest of my cowboy outfit, but my mother had insisted I must be well dressed to travel by train; she said I could change just before I got off.

When the train pulled in, Nig Edwards, the conductor, examined the pass I handed him. Then he told the porter to take good care of me, for the Circle C shipped a lot of cattle over the Great Northern.

When the porter had loaded my stuff I handed him the half dollar I'd been holding in my hand. He told me to sit in the men's washroom until he could get me a berth.

The washroom was overcrowded with drummers with open sample cases when I stepped in, and the air was thick with tobacco smoke. I backed out into the narrow passageway where I collided with something big and solid. Just then the train jolted and lurched, and I made a grab at the

14

heavy green curtains of the washroom that swayed back and forth. I held on as my legs went out from under me.

"Watch where you're going, kid," I heard a woman's cricket-shrill voice scolding me. "And let go my skirt, this minute!"

The train jolted again and there was the sound of tearing cloth. The woman let out a screech and slammed me across the side of my head with her pocketbook, knocking off my hat. I let go and made a grab for my hat just as the woman stepped on it.

My left ear was buzzing, and I was down on my hands and knees trying to get my hat. All I could see was a big piano leg in a high-buttoned shoe planted on the crown. Then the leg moved and I grabbed my new hat and scrambled to my feet.

She was the fattest woman I'd ever laid eyes on, with red jowls, and her pudgy hands were trying to fix her green velvet skirt that I'd torn.

I eased around the corner and into the vestibule out of sight. I examined my squashed hat and felt like bawling. My ear felt numb and there was a humming sound inside my head. I sat down on my sacked saddle and re-shaped my hat. I was in behind the piled baggage, not exactly hiding out, but hoping I wouldn't be noticed if the fat lady came hunting me.

When I heard the vestibule door open I ducked down, but it was only the dining car waiter on his first call to dinner. Then I saw a six-foot man in high-heeled alligator boots. He was George Hall, who had once worked for the Circle C outfit and was now a livestock inspector. I was never so glad to see anyone in my life and I stood up so he would notice me.

There was a grin under his mustache when he said, "Hi, Walt. I was just on my way to supper. Come along."

I wanted to wash up first but I wouldn't go to the wash-room in my car. I told him what had happened, and the way I described the fat lady made George Hall chuckle. "How long has it been since you last saw your Aunt Belle?" he asked, sort of careless.

Aunt Belle and Uncle John Green owned the Shonkin Cattle Company at Fort Benton. I hadn't seen either of them in five years, and said so.

"Your Aunt Belle is a real lady," George said, "and she'll enjoy the joke when the story gets back to her."

The train commenced picking up speed. Aunt Belle would be getting off at Fort Benton, and while I thought a lot of her and knew her heart was as big as the rest of her, still I didn't want to get trapped with her again, so I said I'd wash up in the next car. I filled the basin with water and shoved my head and face into it. By the time I dried off and combed my hair I felt better. I was hungry when I walked to the dining car with the stock inspector.

My berth was made up when I got back to the pullman, my saddle and valise were on the upper bunk of the section. I'd said good-by to George Hall. He was getting off at Havre to look over a carload of Wyoming horses, and per-haps arrest the two horse thieves who were fixing to peddle them.

I crawled into bed and fastened the curtains back and raised the blind as high as it would go. I liked to watch

16

the people on the platform as the train stopped to take on passengers, wondering a little about them. I liked to watch the brakeman swing his lantern as the train jerked and moved on into the night, past the red and green signal lights. And then there was nothing to see except the dark with a far-off light from a ranch house window.

My imagination ran wild, to years ahead when I would be grown and riding across the sky line to see what it looked like somewhere that I'd never been. I could be an outlaw, with a price on my head, riding the outlaw trail and heading for the Mexican border. Or I could be a drifting cowpuncher, riding the grub line, hunting for a new range.

I lay back on my pillow and thought of a lot of things I wanted to do, most of them wishful dreaming, that I knew would never happen.

I never meant to shut my eyes that night, but I did. I was having a bad dream. Old Brocky, the school principal, was standing over me in the schoolroom, with his whip of twisted rawhide. He was looking at the bronc rider sketches I'd just drawn on the flyleaf of my geography book. He grabbed my shoulder and commenced shaking me. "It's time you. . . ."

I awakened fighting the blankets. The porter was shaking me. "Due in Malta in half an hour," he said as he reached into the upper berth for my stuff.

It was three in the morning and I had the washroom all to myself as I changed into my ranch clothes. I admired myself in the full-length mirror—my Levi's rolled up in a four-inch cuff, the black silk neck handkerchief knotted

17

loosely above the collar of my black sateen shirt, my hat at a cowpuncher slant. The only item I lacked was high-heeled boots and I hoped to own my first pair before the summer ended. Right now I was wearing low shoes with leather laces.

". . . sho' 'nuff young cowboy," I heard the porter say admiringly as he helped me off the train.

CHAPTER TWO

I Learn to Drive a Four-Horse Stage

The cow town of Malta was asleep at this early morning hour. I had to carry my saddle and valise the hundred yard distance to the Malta Hotel, where I'd been told to go.

I wanted to go to the White House, which was a small frame cabin belonging to the Circle C and standing at the far end of the main street, but I had had strict orders to stay away from there and wait for the stage at the Malta Hotel.

The White House was always a fascinating place to me. Used by the outfit as a place to change clothes while in town, it was always littered with discarded clothing, ropes, chaps, pack saddles, harness, guns of all descriptions, shaving mugs and open razors, brass cuspidors, and the stale odor of tobacco smoke. Layers of dirt and cigarette butts covered the pine board floor. The walls and ceiling were bullet scarred. A potbellied stove kept the place warm in the winter months. Tarp-covered bedrolls were spread out on the two white-painted iron beds.

Nobody had ever been known to give the White House a thorough house cleaning. It would have taken a team and slip scraper to dig it out. I knew the bloodstained spot on the littered floor where a tinhorn gambler had been shot and killed in a gun duel. There was an ugly, sordid story behind the gun fight between the tinhorn and a cow-puncher over a woman.

The hotel lobby was empty when I went in. The night clerk, who was also the bartender on the graveyard shift, was asleep in a chair behind the bar, his sock feet on a beer keg and a newspaper spread over his face. Every time he snored it rustled the paper.

A round hand bell stood beside the inkstand on the desk near the hotel register, and a couple of pens were shoved into a raw potato. The door opening from the lobby into the barroom was propped open by a brick sewed up in a piece of old carpet.

I tiptoed into the barroom and looked around. There were a lot of old bullet holes in the ceiling where the cow-punchers had shot off their six-shooters. I'd heard it said that a man could spread his bedroll on the floor of the room above the bar free of charge if he wanted to risk the .45 slugs.

The dining room doors opened at five so I sat in the lobby where I could keep an eye on my outfit and watch the clock. I knew that Harry Glover, the stage driver, ate breakfast at the hotel so I figured on eating with him.

When Harry came in and saw me he grinned and slapped me on the back. I told him quickly that I wanted to sit up front with him and learn to drive the four-horse team.

I was glad when he said he had no other passengers this morning. If there had been a woman passenger, and she was halfway good looking, she'd get to sit on the driver's seat. I knew that lady-killer, Harry Glover, from way back.

After breakfast I loaded my stuff in the leather boot at

20

the back of the stage. We stopped at the post office to pick up the mail sacks before leaving town. Then we stopped at the halfway stage station, called the Hog Ranch, for noon dinner and a change of horses. It was almost five in the evening when we topped the hill that looked down on the home ranch.

It looked like a small cow town. My father's white frame house, and my older half brother Wallace's two-storied house, with the Indian skin tepee in the front yard and a huge pile of buffalo skulls, were near the front gate. The two log houses about a hundred yards apart were where my other two half brothers Will and Bob lived. The long low-roofed log bunkhouse, the mess cabin and kitchen and a small whitewashed log cabin between. The buggy house and cow shed and corral. The big high-loft log barn, a storehouse, blacksmith shop and wagon shed, and several other small cabins. About twenty buildings all told.

The pole corral was large enough to hold the remuda of three hundred head of horses. Beaver Creek ran behind the scattered-out buildings, but you couldn't see it for the tall willows and old cottonwoods. Behind it were the winter cattle sheds and corrals.

At this time of the year everything was green. The wild rose bushes made pink splotches against the green willow thickets. The alfalfa field was about a mile long and reached to the Fort Belknap Indian Reservation fence. The alfalfa was in bloom and looked like a giant purple and green carpet from the hill.

A couple of miles to the south were the twin Coburn

Buttes, thick timbered with scrub pine. The Little Rockies lay to the west toward the Reservation.

Looking down on it, with the sun lowering toward the mountains, it was a cattleman's paradise. This was the Circle C home ranch where a part of me had taken root, young roots that went deep and were there to stay.

I was handling the lines as we started down the easy slope of the hill. Harry Glover cut a quick look at my gloved hands to make sure I had each line taut like he'd showed me—lead line over my forefinger, wheel line between the third and little finger of my right hand, and the same with my left hand for the nigh leader and wheeler. That way, I could jerk or loosen each line without shifting my hands, using only the wrists.

Glover wasn't giving me time to get scared. His whiplash hissed like a snake and the popper cracked over the ears of the lead team. When the four horses hit the collars they were in a high lope. Glover slacked his foot off the long brake beam and we were off to the races.

He had cautioned me to keep the slack up and even in the four lines and to see that the leaders kept the tugs tight so the wheel horses wouldn't step into the lead bars; to see that each horse kept pulling his share of the load. I knew that a horse could tell by the feel of the bit in his mouth if a green hand was driving, and that he would be quick to take advantage and try to outsmart a green hand.

At the foot of the hill the leaders quit the road for a split second to keep the lead bars and stretcher bars up and level before they swung back. The old Concord stagecoach lurched sideways, and the leather springs creaked and squealed as we made the turn on two wheels. My short legs were braced against the wooden cowl as I pulled back on the lines, my heart in my throat, and my eyes glued to the leaders. Then the coach righted itself and came back on four wheels.

For the next two hundred yards it was straight road to the ranch. The whip in Glover's hand cracked. I sawed on the lines and pulled the team down to a slow lope, then a high trot as Glover braked. Dust boiled up as the braked rear wheels slid like sled runners in the deep dust-filled ruts.

I pulled to a stop in front of the log office, slacked off the lines in my cramped hands and handed them over to Glover. All of a sudden I felt shaky and weak-kneed. I knew he had risked crippling the horses in a pile up by letting a half-baked kid drive.

I had just taken my saddle and valise out of the boot when I caught sight of my father coming from the cookhouse. He was a short-statured man, with iron-gray hair and mustache and trimmed beard. He had been a powerful man for his size in his youth. Now in his early sixties and shrunken a little, he walked with a cane.

My father was a pioneer who had come to Montana Territory in the early sixties, to follow the gold rush into Virginia City. He had staked out placer claims and had put his gold into cattle and land. He had been one of the Montana Vigilantes who had strung up Henry Plummer and his gang of road agents. He built up one of the biggest cow outfits in Montana.

My three older half brothers, Will, Bob, and Wallace, were grown men now. They ran the Circle C ranch with

23

the help of Horace Brewster, who ramrodded the outfit and had been with my father since he started in the cow business. He taught my brothers all they knew about cattle and horses when they had been my age, just like he took me under his wing during summer vacations.

The twenty year gap or more between myself and my brothers seemed to grow wider. They had learned the cow business the hard way and they took turns loading the work on me; all except Wallace, the youngest of the three, who treated me as a sort of side pardner. Wallace was for many years the crack shot in Montana with rifle or shotgun, a big game hunter who was forever away from the ranch on a hunting trip or trapshooting meet.

My mother and sisters lived in Great Falls. Like the wives and daughters of a lot of cattlemen, they wanted no part of ranch life. When I said good-by to my mother in Great Falls, she never expected to get a letter from me during the three months I would spend on the ranch. Let some cowpuncher catch me writing a letter home and I'd never hear the last of it. A cowboy tied to mama's apron strings, I'd be wanting a hot bath every night, next thing, or somebody to saddle my horse. They would have joshed the life out of me. The only news my mother expected to hear about me would be when my father made one of his frequent trips to Great Falls.

There were no women around the ranch to see to it that I washed behind my ears every time I sat down to a meal. I washed my hands at an outside tin basin and dried them on a roller towel, and sat on a long bench at the table with the rest of the cowpunchers. There were no napkins to fold and roll into napkin rings, and no older sisters to watch my table manners and try to teach me what they had learned at boarding school. It was like the song Wallace used to sing:

> "Out upon the roundup,
> I'll tell you what they eat,
> A li'l' ol' hunk of dry bread
> And a tough ol' chunk of meat,
> A cup of black coffee
> With sugar on the sly,
> And when the cook hollers 'grub pile'
> It's root, hog, or die!"

My father was a stern man who had his own strict code and lived up to it. A fearless man, he went unarmed in a frontier country where most men packed guns, claiming guns got a lot of good men into trouble. He had never laid an angry hand on any of his children but I was always a little in awe of his stern ways. He never demanded the respect due him, but he got it from his sons and every cow hand who ever worked for the Circle C.

He could say more in one short sentence than any man I ever knew. Without sarcasm, he laid down his laws in that many short words. It always wound up in a handshake, my father's way of sealing a bargain. Once I gave my word to him, I never broke it, but at times I bent it almost to the breaking point.

My father put his arm across my shoulder and I felt his hand tighten on my arm. "That white pony of yours is in the barn, eating his head off," he told me. "I reckon you want to see how he wintered."

Snowflake was the white pony my brother Wallace had given me when I was six. I had learned to ride on him. He belonged to me, the only mount in my one-horse string. Snowflake was what was called an easy keeper. I had never seen him when he wasn't slick and fat and in good shape.

I tried not to let on how anxious I was to see Snowflake but I almost broke out of a fast walk into a run as I headed for the barn.

It had been a long nine months since Snowflake had heard the sound of my voice, but when I called his name he pulled his head out of the manger and looked around. I could tell by the way he nuzzled my face and hair that he knew me and was glad to see me back.

He had shed his long winter coat and looked like he had just been sprayed with whitewash. Somebody had curry-combed and brushed his long tail because there wasn't a snarl in it.

I rubbed behind his short furry ears and whispered nonsense in his ear while he enjoyed the unexpected feed of oats I gave him.

I found Horace Brewster behind the barn greasing the wheels of the buckboard. He wiped the axle grease off and shook hands with me. He was getting ready to drive to the Fort Belknap Indian Reservation tomorrow to see about cattle permits, and he invited me to go along.

In my book Horace Brewster was the best all-around cow hand and roundup boss that ever lived, and that opinion was shared by most cowmen and cowhands. I was lucky to learn the cow business under his guidance. He handled me with a hackamore, while my brothers Bob and Will used a spade bit.

I offered to help him grease the buggy but he said he was about finished.

Joe Contway, a short, stocky-built half-breed with a lot of gray in his coarse black hair, came up leading a pair of matched bays. Their sleek coats shone like dark mahogany that had been polished with a waxed cloth.

"This is the matched pair of registered colts your father bought from Old Man Tucker," Brewster told me. "Contway's been breaking 'em out slow and easy under your father's critical eye."

Brewster told me they were named Nip and Tuck and that my father had already matched them in a race against my brother Bob's Lewis and Clark team and my brother Will's Roulette and Faro team. The race would take place about a month from now when the Tucker bays were broke and conditioned to travel the forty-five mile distance from the ranch to Malta. Brewster was going to try them out on a road trip tomorrow morning.

The bay three-year olds were half brothers, sired by the same big bay stud that Old Man Tucker had bought from the racing stables of Senator W. A. Clark of Butte. They were out of different Clark mares, each of which had held the harness racing record in her prime. Nip and Tuck were registered, with a pedigree a mile long.

"By rights, Brewster," Joe Contway said as we followed him into the barn, "I should have a couple more weeks working these colts out around the ranch. They're not ready for the road yet."

"I agree with you, Joe," Brewster said, "but the Old Gent wants to get them hardened up and in shape. He's got his mind set on winning that race next month. Claims road work is the only way to train a team; it gets them used to looking through the bridle at a long stretch of road. A young horse can get barn sour, Joe."

"If it was anybody but you," Contway grumbled, "I wouldn't let Nip and Tuck outa my sight. They're too hot-blooded yet to be trusted. You'll have to watch them every second. It's fly time and their tails will keep switching. Let a rein get under one of their tails, they'll kick the buck-board into kindling wood."

Joe Contway was still muttering to himself as he got busy with currycomb and brush. He was the best in the country when it came to breaking a colt. Even-tempered, soft spoken around a green bronc, he worked easily at first, without any abrupt motion that might spook a colt unused to a man's ways. Later on, when the colt got used to the handler's smell and accustomed to his movements, the trainer could afford to get a little careless.

The supper bell rang and we headed for the cookhouse to wash up.

When I bedded down that night I was as happy as a ranch kid could be after a long winter's schooling. I welcomed the thought of getting up before daylight to wrangle the horse pasture, which was my job. I went to sleep with that chore in mind.

CHAPTER THREE

The Runaway

Joe Contway and a ranch hand held the Tucker bays while Brewster and I climbed into the buckboard. Brewster pulled down his hat and slid the buggy whip out of the socket. The bays reared and lunged into the collars when the men let go the bits. Brewster held his foot on the brake, the locked hind wheels sliding in the dust.

When we passed the office door where my father was standing Brewster raised the whip in a sort of salute and my father returned the salute with his cane.

Brewster kicked off the brake and Nip and Tuck were reaching out on a tight rein. It was a mile to the Reservation gate; by that time he had them settled down to a long distance road trot.

I could tell by the look on his face that he was a little nervous. I was too when I got out to open the wire gate. I was careful to lift it and not to drag it on the ground and scare the team. Brewster told me to let it stay open. Both horses were on their hind legs, rearing to go, when I grabbed the seat and swung aboard.

Contway was a hundred per cent right. The Tucker bays were all set to run away, and this was a bad place to handle a runaway team. A barbwire fence was to the east; ahead lay a nest of small hills and cut coulees, thick with high brush; to the west was Beaver Creek with its high willows and cutbanks.

Brewster cast looks all around for an open stretch where he could bend the team in a wide circle in the hope that they would run themselves out.

I had been over every mile of this stretch of country, and there was only one possible clearing large enough to run down the team in a circle. It was the Indian graveyard on a high flat bench a mile or more from the wagon road we were on.

The Indians buried their dead in pine boxes on top of the ground, as was their custom. Some were placed on platforms made of small poles fastened to four upright posts about ten feet high. Some were in boxes, others wrapped in blankets or canvas tarps tied down with ropes or strips of green rawhide that had dried out a long time ago. They were mostly decorated with red, white and blue bunting, the colors faded and run together from the rains and melting snows. Rags were tied to clumps of brush and fastened to willow sticks. These were the ghost flags to keep the evil spirits away from the dead.

The burial ground was our only chance, a slim one at that.

His face grim, Brewster watched the way the horses' ears were cocked and twitching. He could tell by the feel of the lines that they were waiting for the slightest excuse to take off. Both horses had their tails grabbed—pulled down tight across the rounded leather cruppers that fitted under their tails. I knew that when a horse "grabs its tail" it was a danger sign that meant the haunches were tense as coiled springs, and the animal was ready to lash out behind with both feet.

Brewster was anticipating such a move, and he had the whip out. If he could time it to the second, he'd use the whip. A lash across the rumps would be a swift, sudden surprise. They would jump and run without kicking out behind to smash the rig. A driver who knew his business stood a good chance of winning.

It was like sitting on a moving powder keg with the fuse sputtering.

The whip whistled, then came down with a quick back and forth lash across the rumps of both horses. I was sure that all four buckboard wheels left the ground as the bays snorted and broke into a run.

We were across the brushy coulee and going up the slant in nothing flat. It was a typical Indian road to the high bench, just a couple of grass-grown parallel ruts going straight up.

Brewster kept the whip cutting the air a foot or so above the horses' backs, and he held a tight rein. We topped the rise and flattened out on level ground, keeping a safe distance from the edge of the slope. His eyes never left the running team.

In the broad middle of the cemetery was a newly erected platform set on pine poles. It held the body of a dead Indian wrapped in a red blanket, and surrounding the corpse were his personal belongings.

Bunched under the platform, the squaws sat in a tight circle, blankets pulled across their heads, ashes rubbed in their hair and faces. The bucks moved in a slow circle around the platform, never lifting their moccasined feet off the ground. The drummer was squatted against an upright pole with a painted drum in his lap. The faces of the men were streaked with black, yellow and red paint.

Above the rattle of the buckboard wheels I could hear the slow beat of the drum and the sound of the death chant.

It spooked the horses. Brewster kept sawing on the lines to keep them from clamping down and cold-jawing the broken snaffle bits.

The mourners at the burial ceremony gave no sign that they had seen us, but two Indian policemen rode toward us on painted horses. The older one was bareheaded, his long hair parted and hanging down in braids. The younger one's hair was cut like a white man's, and he wore a high-crowned, wide-brimmed black hat. They wore blue uniform coats with brass buttons stamped with the American Eagle. The sun caught the reflection of the badges pinned to their coats. They had policemen's clubs belted on, and Winchester carbines in saddle scabbards.

They looked like a pair of life-sized sentinels put there to block the road. You could see them trying to puzzle out some rule or regulation to put us under arrest for this unusual, unheard-of breach of reservation law.

The Tucker bays must have gotten their second wind. It would take a high solid stone wall to stop them.

Brewster swung his weight on the left line. By a scant margin the runaway rig missed the pair of Indian policemen who stood tracked in the middle of the road. We were on our second lap, leaving a strung-out dust cloud behind.

The drum beat louder, the dismal chant swelled and rolled across the graveyard, eerie and blood chilling. The squaws swayed back and forth, the bucks shuffled and stomped to the dull thunder of the drum beats.

Brewster had a cold-jawed team in his gloved hands. The horses were spooked and all they wanted to do now was to outrun that nameless terror. They headed across the graveyard. A high platform loomed up ahead. There was a sickening crash of splintered wood and I ducked my head by instinct.

The hub of the rear wheel on my side hit a pole and snapped it like a match, slamming the rig sideways. The rear wheel on the driver's side struck another pole, chopping it down like a double-bitted axe. The horses were terror-crazed in a headlong getaway. The heavy crash behind us was Old Chief Set 'Em High in his bunting-wrapped box coming down to earth. He had been up there for twelve or fifteen years.

We slid past between a low picket fence and Old Watches The Moon's box that was roped to a homemade bobsled, and headed straight for the high-wheeled Red River cart that held the boxed bones of Many Sleeps. The dished wheel on my side collapsed, the iron tire bounced high and caromed off at high speed, straight for the drummer and the chanting mourners.

The rear end of the rig on my side went thudding down, the hub with the broken spokes plowing a deep furrow as the buckboard rode on its rear axle. We skinned past

33

the Red River cart so close I could have reached out and touched it for good luck. We needed it. There was nothing to stop us now.

I cut a quick look over my shoulder as a wild, clamorous shout came from the mourners. The iron tire had missed the drummer by inches and hit the upright pole behind him, bouncing back and then climbing the pole to hang there. We'd hung a ringer for sure.

The hub dragging in the hard packed sod acted as a heavy brake, and Nip and Tuck slowed down to a lope. Brewster sawed on the lines as we headed down from the bench to the road where the two policemen sat their spotted ponies.

We were riding our luck, high, wide and handsome, as we went down the slant and hit the flat road twenty feet below. The axle rough-locked the rig and Brewster had the bays slowed to a road gait by the time we'd traveled a mile. He drove them off the road into the shade of a cottonwood tree and they were ready and willing to call it quits.

Sweat trickled from under Brewster's hat and slid off his face in big drops. He was flexing his gloved hands, a hard bright twinkle in his eyes, and a sickly grin on his mouth.

"It's only a matter of time," his voice was bone-dry, "until those two Indian police make their medicine. The young one is Adam Roan Hoarse who'd throw his own mother in the dallyhouse. But the older one, Likes The Women, doesn't want to make any mistakes. He goes strictly by the book and it'll take him a while to remember something in the rules to fit our crime. Meanwhile, we had better get moving."

34

We found a long pole and fastened it under the rig with halter ropes to hold the rear end up, letting the pole drag. By the time we got underway the bay team had their wind back.

It was a tedious, lengthy ride, that fifteen miles to the subagency. The dragging pole left a yellow ribbon of dust behind us. Brewster said it was just what the Vet ordered for the rollicky Tucker bays. Nip and Tuck had been broken of the bad habit of running away.

We stopped in the middle of Beaver Creek and I walked along the buggy tongue to release the check reins while both horses watered. Then Brewster and I washed the sweat and dirt from our heads and faces and drank our fill before we went on our way.

It was like traveling by automobile with a flat tire. Brewster was thankful the horses weren't crippled. There wasn't a scratch on them; only the white marks of dried sweat.

Looking back on the whole thing we could see the comical side of the runaway, but Brewster was worried because the runaway at the Indian burial ground could prove disastrous to the friendship and good will existing between the Reservation Indians and the cattlemen. The Circle C had a permit to run cattle on the Reservation and any mockery of their religious beliefs was a dangerous thing. The runaway episode had broken into a sacred right.

It was an hour past noon when we got to the subagency at Lodge Pole. We unhooked the team from the damaged buckboard and spent the best part of an hour with brush and currycomb at the log barn. By the time we finished, the mahogany bay coats of Nip and Tuck shone like a pair of new boots.

A tall handsome young half-breed named Charlie Perry was in charge of the store and post office. He'd just finished his freshman year at Haskell University, where he was on the freshman football team. He had on a sweater with his class numeral across the front.

Brewster and I sat on the counter and ate sardines and canned tomatoes and crackers, and listened to Charlie talk about school. We were almost finished when Jim Bolster, the I.D. (Indian Department) ramrod rode up. He swung down and dropped his bridle reins, ground-tying his horse and came in.

Brewster and Jim Bolster were old-time friends but it was the first time I'd met the I.D. wagon boss. I liked him on sight when he shook my hand, treating me like a man.

While Brewster and the I.D. ramrod squatted on their boot heels outside in the shade, with vest-pocket tally books and stub pencils in hand, Charlie Perry measured me for a pair of cowboy boots that Brewster had told him to order for me from the H. C. Hyer Boot Company at Olathe, Kansas.

I took off my shoe and stood with my sock foot on a white piece of writing paper while Perry drew the outline of my foot with an indelible pencil. Then he measured my instep with the tape measure.

When Brewster came in, I tried to thank him. I was bursting with happiness and grinning from ear to ear.

The grin died a slow death when I saw the two Indian police outside. They were examining the buckboard with the pole crutch. We had left a trail that a blind man could follow.

Brewster and I were sure mousetrapped.

We gave Perry a brief account of the fix we were in. Perry said to leave it to him. He went into the storeroom and brought out a brand-new saddle and placed it on a sawhorse.

"Adam Roan Horse wants this saddle," Perry told us. "But he's already on the books for fifty dollars. Horace, pretend you're interested in buying it for the Circle C kid, then turn around and make Adam a present of it. That might just square you."

I looked the saddle over. It was a cheap Eastern mail-order job, strictly for the Indian trade, but I let on that I admired it. Then I straddled it.

Adam Roan Horse came in first. When he saw me in the saddle his lower jaw sagged.

"How, Adam!" said Charlie Perry. "Too bad you couldn't raise the money to buy that saddle."

"You said you'd give me six months to pay," Adam said, disappointment in his voice.

Perry opened the ledger and told Adam he was on the books for the limit of his credit. Then he turned to Brewster and said, "Maybe you could fix it so that Adam Roan Horse could have the saddle, Mr. Brewster, if the Circle C kid is willing to give it up."

I slid from the saddle and held out my hand. "How! Adam Roan Horse!" I knew he liked to be called by his full name. He had gone to the Indian school at Fort Shaw near Great Falls. He was the fattest kid in school, and he looked like that fat, moon-faced kid now, with the sweat-like melted lard on his face, and his eyes dull and sad.

Likes The Women was standing in the doorway, leaning against the door jam. His eyes were fixed on Brewster who was holding up and admiring a string of colored glass beads he'd found on the counter.

"How, Cola!" Brewster motioned him over with the beads. "How, Cola!" he repeated. "How, Friend!"

Perry started talking sign language to Likes The Women. He was using both hands and talking slow enough for me to get a smattering of what he was saying. The speech he was making should admit him to membership in the Liars Club.

He told Likes The Women that the evil spirits had followed the buckboard in a large cloud, then had climbed the backs of the white man's horses like a swarm of horse-flies. The evil spirits, riding the clouds, had guided the team up the steep road to the burial ground. Brewster had tried to drive them off with the buggy whip as he'd circled the runaway team, but no white man's whip could move them. They were after Hold The Skunk who was being buried, and they had used the white man's rig to lead them to the sacred burial ground.

The white man, Perry explained, had to drive fast, risking his life and the boy's when he carried the evil spirits down from the burial ground where they disappeared behind a cloud.

Likes The Women, Perry told him, should shake the hand of the white man who had saved the dead Indian from the evil spirits.

Brewster was surprised when Likes The Women came toward him with his hand held out.

"Make him a present of the beads," Perry whispered. "And give Adam Roan Horse the saddle. I think that'll put you in the clear."

"The saddle is yours, Adam Roan Horse," I said quickly. "The Circle C will make you a present of it."

Likes The Women's face spread in a wide grin as he took the glass beads from Brewster. They shook hands.

Brewster bought them each a five-cent cigar. Adam Roan Horse put the new saddle on his horse, and with the colored beads hung around Likes The Women's neck, they rode away satisfied.

The subagency blacksmith was repairing the buckboard. After Brewster settled with Charlie Perry for the cost of the saddle and the beads, we spread our bedrolls on the floor of the store.

Awake at the rack of dawn, we watered and grained the Tucker bays and hooked them up. We drove to the I.D. roundup camp for breakfast.

We reached the Fort Belknap Agency that afternoon, where Brewster talked to Major Logan and got the cattle grazing permit renewed for the Circle C.

Sundown found us back at the ranch. Brewster drove the Tucker bays past the ranch buildings. They were curried and brushed until their coats shone like polished mahogany. Brewster had Nip and Tuck stepping out like Dan Patch had reached out to win the world's sulky record. He raised the buggy whip as we passed the office where my father and two brothers stood in the doorway, like the driver of Dan Patch had lifted his whip in salute to the judges as he crossed the finish line.

My father lifted his cane, his bearded grin squinting his sky-blue eyes.

CHAPTER FOUR

How I Joined the Wild Bunch

The Fourth of July, coming in the slack months between roundups, gave the cowpunchers a chance to take a day or two off to celebrate. Most of them had shaved and put on their best clothes, saddled their private horses, and pulled out the morning of the third for town.

Roy Long Knife, the horse wrangler, left before breakfast for the three-day Indian dances at Lodge Pole. The wrangler's job was all mine until he got back.

Bob was in charge of the ranch and it looked like I'd have to stay with him. All the hired hands had pulled out except Al Taylor, the ranch cook. My father had gone to Great Falls and so had Will. Wallace had gone to Helena for a rifle match.

I had brought a bunch of firecrackers with me, but tomorrow was going to be a mighty sorry glorious Fourth for me, any way you wanted to look at it.

Bob told me to take the remuda to water on Beaver Creek and let them graze most of the day. I was told to pasture them at a certain place at sundown.

"When you get back to the ranch," Bob promised, "we'll set off some firecrackers I have in my basement. I'll tell Al to freeze some ice cream."

Al fixed a lunch for me and put it and a bottle of coffee

41

in a clean flour sack. I put in a can of tomatoes and a double handful of dried apricots. I took a sack of Bull Durham tobacco from the bunkhouse, and once out of sight of the ranch I put it in my shirt pocket and let the tag with the picture of the bull hang out.

I got a good count on the horses before I let them spread out to graze. Then I rode up on a high knoll where I could keep an eye on them.

When the sun was noon high I bunched the horses and drifted them slowly to water. Then I ate my lunch and rolled a smoke. I took a couple of puffs and when the cigarette went out I let it hang from the corner of my mouth like I'd seen cowpunchers do.

I mounted Snowflake and got a range count on the horses, checking twice to make sure. Then I stripped and went swimming in a deep hole, where an old beaver dam had been torn out.

Later in the afternoon I was feeling disappointed about missing the town celebrations the next day, but there was nothing to be done about it. Toward sundown I bunched the remuda and hazed them toward the horse pasture. It was then I sighted the four horsebackers, split up in pairs about a quarter mile apart, riding at a high trot toward the remuda.

When they saw me they slowed down. One pair came on while the other pair split up and stayed on the hill on lookout. Then one of the first pair dropped behind and only one rider came on.

I had a notion they might be horse thieves on the prowl,

and when I saw the carbine the man had across his lap I knew I was up against something dangerous.

He rode slowly around the outer edge of the remuda and came toward where I sat Snowflake at the corner gate. As he came closer I tried to make out his face but couldn't for the black whiskers. His white teeth showed in the black mask; it could have been meant for a grin, or it could have been something else. His hat was slanted across his eyes, and he wore a cartridge belt and six-shooter.

I was more excited than scared. If they were horse thieves there wasn't much I could do about it. A fourteen-year-old with a jackknife couldn't put up much of a fight against four heavily armed men.

The black-whiskered man pulled up. He called me by name, then said, "Jimmer says you know how to keep your mouth shut." He shoved the Winchester 30-30 into the saddle scabbard and unbuckled the strap that held his ketch-rope.

Jimmer was Jim Thornhill, a nearby rancher and close family friend.

I said, "Yes, sir." I had a good notion who he was.

"Our horses are played out," he said as he stood in the stirrups and motioned with the coiled rope for the others to come on. "We're travelin' light and borrowin' the loan of some Circle C horses." He shook out a loop in the rope. Then he cautioned me. "When you get back to the ranch, just remember you ain't seen nobody. You didn't see anyone take any horses. It never happened. You get the idea?" he asked.

43

"I keep my mouth shut," I said, trying to keep my voice steady.

"If a two-bit sheriff and his posse show up at the ranch, remember you never saw me. You don't know a thing," he warned me again.

"Yes, sir. I keep my mouth shut."

He grinned, then said, "Ride that white pony up on that little pinniwankle. If you see any horsebackers acomin', ride around in a tight circle, then hightail it for home."

I did like he told me. There was no sign of any horsebackers. I saw the four riders bunch the remuda in the corner of the fence and hold them without choucing them around. One by one they roped a fresh mount, and quickly changed horses.

The black-whiskered man waved me down as the four rode off at a high trot. There was not a sign that they had been there except the four sweat-marked horses they'd left. All of them were in Jim Thornhill's Seven Up brand.

I opened the gate and eased the horses into the pasture.

My pulse beat inside my throat. I wasn't scared, just keyed up. I had a right to be, for I knew who the black-whiskered rider was. He was Harvey Logan, alias Kid Curry. I had seen one of the handbills with his name and description and the amount of the reward for his capture, dead or alive. I knew that the other three outlaws were all members of the notorious Wild Bunch.

Every ranch kid in the Little Rockies knew every wild tale there was to tell about Kid Curry. Every kid wanted to pattern his ways after the outlaw, but none except the Thornhill boys, Harvey and Bill, had ever actually seen

Kid Curry. The Thornhill boys never talked about the outlaw, who was their father's partner in the ranch and after whom the oldest boy was named. They knew how to keep their mouths shut, and Jimmer had told Kid Curry that I was the same way, closemouthed.

I'd always dreamed about joining the Wild Bunch someday, and now today, right this evening, that wishful dreaming had come true. Kid Curry himself had sent me up on the hill as lookout. I was actually one of the gang. Talk about excitement; this was it. I held a secret that was far beyond anything I had ever dared hope for. And nothing, nothing this side of death, could ever get me to say or hint one word that would unlock that secret.

Much as I respected my father, he would never know what happened during that short half hour at sundown.

Kid Curry had mentioned a sheriff and posse. Well, that sheriff would never get a word out of me.

I was a full-fledged outlaw, one of the Wild Bunch, that evening as I rode Snowflake back to the ranch.

I wondered what Kid Curry and the other members of the Wild Bunch had been up to; what bank they had robbed. I remembered the bulge in the Kid's slicker tied behind the cantle of his saddle, the wide cartridge belt with every loop filled, and the leg of a boot, sewn at the bottom, bulging with 30-30 cartridges, that hung from his saddle horn.

There was nobody at the barn when I rode up and unsaddled. I tied Snowflake in an empty stall and fed him an extra lard pail of oats, filled the manger with hay and bedded the stall.

Bob's private horse was in its stall, fed and bedded.

It was long past suppertime when I got to the cook shack. Al Taylor told me that Bob wanted me to go over to his house as soon as I finished eating. "What's he caught you in this time?" Al asked seriously.

I had a few bad moments wondering what I'd done until I remembered the fireworks Bob had in his basement. I wolfed my food and polished off two bowls of ice cream, then high-tailed it for Bob's house.

He was sitting in the front room with a newspaper, smoking one of his small cigars when I came in. "You didn't go to sleep and spill the remuda, did you?" Bob asked.

"I tallied them when I put them in the pasture," I assured him, which was the truth. I didn't mention that four Circle C horses were gone and replaced by four Seven Up horses.

"It's still a little early for the fireworks," Bob said. "Get a book and read awhile." He went back to his newspaper.

I pretended to read, but all the time I wondered what was up. Bob seemed to be waiting for something to happen and I shared that uneasiness.

Then we heard the horsebackers. It sounded like a lot of them and they were stopping at the hitchrack out front.

Bob was suddenly on his feet, looking big and tough with his black scowl, his hard steel-gray eyes narrowed. He wore a coat and I knew he had a gun shoved inside the waistband of his pants.

There was the heavy tromp of boots on the porch and a loud hammering on the door. "See who it is," Bob said quietly. He turned the lampwick down a little.

46

The front room had folding doors leading into the hall-way. I opened them just wide enough to go through. I slid the inside bolt and opened the door.

The big man on the porch shoved it open the rest of the way. I saw the sheriff's badge pinned to his unbuttoned vest, a wide filled cartridge belt sagging across his middle. I didn't like his looks. I didn't like anything about him.

"Who's here besides you, Kid?"

I didn't answer. I stood in his way, the top of my head level with the law badge. He'd have to shove me aside to get in.

My brother came into the hall. "I'm Bob Coburn," he said. "What do you want?"

"I'm the sheriff," the officer said gruffly. "Kid Curry and his gang held up the Great Northern train at Wagner. I'm hot on their trail. I want supper and fresh horses for my posse of twenty-five men."

Bob gripped my shoulder. "Go to the cookhouse and tell Al Taylor he doesn't have to feed these men, but if he feels like it he can fix them supper and charge them a dollar a head. Tell him to collect in advance."

He told the sheriff, "You're afoot as far as Circle C horses are concerned. If you want a place to sleep, there's plenty of hills to bed down on." Bob slammed the door shut and slid the bolt.

"You better go out the back door and tell Al what I said." His voice was tight and his eyes dangerous. If the sheriff had spoken out of turn or made a move for his gun, I knew Bob would have been on top of him, and from

47

what I'd heard Bob was a hard man to stop once he got started.

He let me out the back door and I heard him bolt it. I was at the cookhouse in nothing flat. When I gave Al Bob's message and told him about the train robbery, he said, "Where I came from a lawman usually gave the orders. When he said jump, you stepped lively."

I told him this was different. This was the Circle C and Kid Curry had worked for the outfit, as well as his brothers Lonny and Johnny. The sheriff had come to the wrong place to demand favors that would help him catch the Kid.

I was pretty sure by now that Kid Curry had made arrangements for the getaway change of horses and that's why Bob had sent me out with the remuda and told me where to pasture them at sundown. But I said nothing about that to Al.

The sheriff made out an order on Valley County, where he came from, for the supper Al was cooking and putting on the table. While they ate I stayed in the kitchen, listening to what they said.

The sheriff told Al that he'd sent out a mess wagon and bed wagon and fifty head of horses, but somehow the wagons and remuda had gotten lost. He had told Tim Maloney to follow the stage road and he couldn't figure out how they could get lost in broad daylight.

What the sheriff didn't know, and I did, was that Tim Maloney was a good friend of the Curry boys. It looked to me like he had gotten lost on purpose.

I got a bird's-eye view of the workings of a sheriff's posse during the following two weeks that they spent hunting the train robbers who had held up the Great Northern train at two o'clock in the afternoon of July 3, 1901.

The sheriff and his men turned their played-out horses in the lower pasture. They were afoot, and they stayed afoot most of the next day.

It was a strange sort of Fourth of July. For all its quiet on the surface, there were plenty of fireworks ready to explode.

News in the cow country travels like a prairie fire blown by a strong wind. The cowpunchers who had gone to town commenced drifting back in pairs, and every man had a six-shooter stuck in the waistband of his pants. Down to the last man, they were all on the side of the train robbers. Like the Circle C, they had all been Kid Curry's friend.

Some of the sheriff's poolroom posse had set up a target. They were bombarding it when Bob showed up and put a stop to the shooting. He told the sheriff that the Circle C cowpunchers were drifting back to the ranch, and that they had all punched cows with the Curry boys. Let one of the posse talk out of turn and there would be a ruckus that nothing could stop.

Right from the start the sheriff had been asking for trouble when he'd ridden up so highhanded with his demands. He couldn't have picked a worse place than the Circle C ranch, and by now he was beginning to realize his bad move.

When the stage drove in, Harry Glover had some important passengers—a U. S. Postal Inspector and two detectives hired by the railroad company. Glover called them Pinkerton men.

49

Around noon or a little later the posse's horse wrangler showed up with the horses. He said Tim Maloney had camped the wagons just inside the reservation fence where the stage road crossed Beaver Creek.

By the time the sheriff and his men got saddled up and on their way, they were following an almost twenty-four hour cold trail.

The dust of the departing posse settled in the Fourth of July sunset. With it came an uneasy quiet, like the lull before a storm. The two Pinkerton detectives were still at the ranch and so was the postal inspector. I wondered what would happen if I was to touch off a bunch of firecrackers after dark. Holy cow! They'd pile out of the bunkhouse and office with guns apoppin'. It gave me goose-pimples to even think about it.

When I finally went to bed I lay on my bunk, with an ear cocked, wide-awake and thinking of all that had happened, listening to any outside sounds, until I fell asleep from sheer exhaustion.

The following two weeks I rode fence with Humpy Jack Davis, the nighthawk. We pulled out after breakfast and came back at suppertime, each packing a sack of staples and a short-handed claw hammer.

Around noon time we would strip and swim in the Rolling M reservoir or in Beaver Creek, wherever we happened to be. After our swim we would eat a packed lunch of canned tomatoes and some crackers and cheese. Then we'd take five in the shade.

Jack Davis was hawk-beaked and lean-jawed and red-headed, with the long legs and arms of a six-footer. Above the belt he was hunchbacked. He had been crippled in a nasty pile up on the Tanforan Track in California when he was a top jockey and in his prime. He was in his late thirties now, and while he was bent over and crippled for life, he was the best nighthawk in the cow country and the best four-horse-team skinner anywhere. In a free-for-all ruckus Jack Davis was a wildcat to handle.

He was sensitive about his deformity. Few men ever saw him without a shirt on, but he didn't seem to mind exposing his back to me. During those few weeks, while we lived the life of Riley, we built up a friendship that lasted through the years.

Every evening when we got back to the ranch, we picked up the latest news of the sheriff's posse. They were still camped in the neighborhood cutting for sign of the train robbers.

About the time that the posse gave up the manhunt and went back to town, I sighted the four Circle C horses that had been "borrowed" by the outlaws. They were back in the remuda, and the four Seven Up geldings were missing that same morning.

The two Pinkerton men and the United States postal inspector finally gave up and left the ranch.

CHAPTER FIVE

Bronco Breaking

The cow country was still talking about the train robbery
when Charlie Brewster showed up at the ranch to break a
string of two- and three-year old broncs that Joe Contway
had just finished halter breaking.

Horace Brewster's brother Charlie was, according to a
lot of men who were good judges of broncs and riders, one
of the wildest bronc stompers in any man's country.

He had no fear of any horse, and the way he handled
himself around a green colt, you would think he was working a broken horse that was acting playful.

There was all the difference in the world in the way
Joe Contway and Charlie Brewster handled a green colt.
Contway was soft-spoken, easy going, patient, gentle man-
nered around a horse. Charlie Brewster wasted no time
about it; he would simply front foot a bronc and get him
blindfolded, then put the saddle on and pull the cinch
tight while the horse stood with a hump in his back.

Charlie would then ease into the saddle, a quirt in his
hand. When he had both feet in the stirrups he's tell Contway to slack the rope on the front legs. Like as not he
would be grinning and have a half-smoked cigarette in the
corner of his mouth when he reached along the horse's

neck and jerked off the blindfold. From then on it was kitty-bar-the-door.

If the bronc sulled and refused to pitch, Charlie would rake his spur rowels along the neck and shoulders and back along the ribs and flanks to get the results he wanted.

To his way of thinking, easy handling babied a colt along. If the colt didn't get the buck out of him at the start, one day when a cowboy wasn't expecting it, that too-easily handled horse would come apart and the cowboy would eat a mouthful of dirt and be set afoot forty miles from nowhere.

Charlie Brewster and Joe Contway had practically grown up together. They punched cows for the same outfits, each man riding his rough string of broncs, each according to his own way. Their arguments around the roundup camps and bunkhouses about the correct way to handle a colt were lengthy and endless.

There was a purpose in Horace Brewster pairing off his wild brother Charlie with Joe Contway. Horace could see the good points and the bad to both methods of handling a green bronc.

The twenty head of big stout colts waiting to be broken were all sired by the same stud, an iron-gray stallion that was half Percheron, half Morgan. The brood mares were a wide assortment of quarter horses, Steeldust stock, a few from the Crow Reservation and some from the Piegan Reserve. There were half a dozen Apaloosa mares from the Palouse country in Idaho, and a few thoroughbred mares and some Cleveland bays.

And while the big iron-gray stud marked his get of sire,

each colt had a strain of its mother's blood, each an individual with its own traits, according to the blood lines.

I helped the two bronc busters corral the horses and I wanted to help in the handling of them, but I knew that bronc handling could be dangerous to a fourteen-year-old who was apt to get underfoot, doing more harm than good.

I was tickled to death when Horace Brewster said I could make myself useful by opening and closing the gates.

Next morning after breakfast I rode Snowflake up to the corrals where the broncs were milling around. There were two large corrals and a smaller one where the broncs were to be ridden on their first saddling.

Both bronc riders were mounted on big stout rope horses and I opened the gate to one of the large corrals and let them in. I was told to leave my pony where he wouldn't get chouched around, and that suited Snowflake.

The first day was spent roping the colts, getting the halters on and leading each one around the empty corral, with a long rope dallied around a saddle horn. It was hot, dusty work, with the colt fighting the rope, throwing himself at times, to lie in the dust, blowing, dripping sweat, sulled.

It was my job to get him to his feet. I'd whack him across the rump with a ten-foot doubled rope, or I'd grab his tail and lift. Sometimes I had to move fast.

We left six broncs tied up when the dinner bell sounded. "Give 'em time to think it over," Charlie Brewster said, wiping the sweat off.

When I closed the gate and looked for Snowflake, he wasn't there. He had gotten tired of waiting and had sneaked off. He was probably back in the barn eating hay. I got on behind Joe Contway and rode down the hill. Sure enough Snowflake was inside his stall with a manger full of hay.

When he saw me, he rolled an eye and flattened both ears back. He lifted one hind foot like he was going to kick my teeth out. When I grabbed his hoof he set it down fast, and I couldn't keep from laughing, he was such a fraud. I loosened the saddle cinch and took off his bridle.

After dinner we rode back to the corrals and led the loose broncs out to water at the creek, then back to the corrals. The two bronc stompers led the six tied colts to water and whenever one of them sulled and fought the rope I whipped him from behind. They were led into the barn and tied up, and I shoveled hay from the loft into the mangers. Then I followed the two men to the corrals.

Charlie Brewster spotted a couple of broncs that he said were "snakes," and he aimed to handle them according to the way he figured they needed working. One was a big hammer-headed, rat-tailed Apaloosa with a dozen big white spots scattered on his black rump.

I held the gate open while Charlie and Contway hazed him into an empty corral. Charlie roped him and choked him down. The bronc threw himself, and Joe Contway sat on his neck and held him down till Brewster got him saddled on the ground.

When the saddle was cinched down Contway eased the hackamore over his head while Charlie stood straddle of the horse and rolled a cigarette. When the hackamore was in place, Charlie took the rope in one hand and reached down to grab the saddle horn. "I got 'im, Joe," he said, letting the smoke drift from his nose. "Let 'im up."

Contway got off the sweaty neck and stepped back quickly. The Apaloosa rolled the white of an eye at the man standing straddle of him, then he swung his head back and whistled and came up on all four legs like they were springs.

Charlie threw his weight in one stirrup and yanked his slaunchwise saddle straight by its horn.

The big bronc squealed and reared up on his hind legs, pawing the air. I sucked in my breath and held it as the horse came over backwards. I saw Charlie kick both feet out of the stirrups, while he grabbed a handful of black mane.

There was a heavy dull thud as man and horse came over backwards in the dust. All you could see as the dust billowed around them was a tangle of horse's legs kicking and striking in all directions. Then the bronc came up with Charlie straddle of him. Charlie had lost his hat but the cigarette still hung in a sideways grin.

The bronc stood stiff-legged, whistling through red flared nostrils, with a hump in his back like a camel. Then he squatted and tried it a second time. Charlie let him get almost straight up, then he let him have it. He brought the heavy shot-loaded quirt down between the bronc's ears. The Apaloosa shook his head from side to side, then he came down forward this time, and went to his knees.

He stayed on his knees for quite a while, his head hanging down and swinging from side to side, while Charlie just sat there, sort of sideways in the saddle, waiting.

The bronc came up fighting and Charlie kept the rope slack while he chinned the moon. He had all the tricks of the bucking trade in his system and he used them all, one at a time. He swapped ends like he was turning inside out in his spotted hide, then he spun like a top in a tight circle.

The bronc rider kicked his jaw and straightened the kink out of his limber neck, then he came up from the ground sideways, sunfishing, all four legs clear as if he were sailing at a flat angle. Then he landed limber-legged and almost somersaulted till he got his balance.

He stood there, legs spread, whistling, while he got bunched for another try. Then he grabbed his tail and his head went down between his front legs and he tried several high, long jumps. Every time his hoofs hit the ground he landed hard and heavy, as if he meant to jar the rider's brains loose. On the third jump, Charlie's nose spurted blood. The bronc bucked headlong into the big pole gate and cracked the middle poles. Horse and rider went down in a heavy puff of dust and it looked to me like the bronc rolled over, but he was back on his feet so fast I couldn't tell for sure.

Charlie had lost his right stirrup but his foot caught it on the second jump the bronc made. Finally he quit pitching and his head came up and he crowhopped alongside the corral fence so close it scarred the rider's stirrup and scraped the fringe from the worn leather chaps.

Charlie let the horse travel like that, twice around the corral. His face looked gray under the dust and sweat and the blood that came from his nose and both ears. His white teeth showed in a ghastly grin and the cigarette stub hung glued in a corner of his mouth.

"Fork your horse, Joe," Charlie told Contway in a croaking voice. "Open the gate, kid. This dust is gettin' bad."

I swung the gate open. When the Apaloosa saw the gap he charged out at a run. Contway was alongside, hazing the bronc and rider across the prairie in a straight line, like a matched horse race. A hundred yards and they were out of sight in a long draw.

I let out my breath and commenced breathing once more. It seemed like a long time before the two horse-backers came in sight, the Apaloosa slowed down to a sullen, dogged trot. As they neared the corral Charlie dropped his horsehair reins across the saddle horn and reached into the pocket of his torn dirty, blood-spattered shirt for his sack of tobacco and cigarette papers.

"It's horses like this big Injun," he grinned and spat out blood and dirt, "that make a bronc stomper's life worth the livin'."

And that's how the Apaloosa bronc got his Big Injun name.

Charlie washed the blood and dirt off and lazed in the shade of the corral while Joe Contway roped out a short-coupled iron-gray two-year-old that both men agreed showed the Steeldust quarter horse strain. Contway said he was out of a little Piegan black mare the Indians must have stolen from some Texas wagon train outfit.

Bronc riders have the privilege of naming the horses they break, and Joe Contway called the chunky built iron-gray,

Moss Agate. He weighed about 850 pounds and was just under fourteen hands high.

Moss Agate was two and he would block out some but wouldn't grow any taller. "Just the right size for you," Contway told me. "I'll tell Horace to sorta sleeper-mark Moss Agate for your string of horses next summer. By the time I'm finished with this colt you'll be able to turn him on a dime and get a nickle change. Bein' he's going to be yours, you might as well have a hand in breakin' him."

I helped Contway put the halter on and we turned him loose in the small corral to let him drag the hair rope around for awhile. Contway squatted on his boot heels and rolled a smoke, watching the colt circle the corral. Finally he told me to have a go at him.

I worked him on foot. In a half hour I had him to where I could lead him without much trouble. Then Contway told me he was ready to be sacked-out.

I used a worn-out old saddle blanket that smelled of horse sweat. Holding the hackamore rope in one hand and the blanket in the other, I rubbed the sweat and dust off the colt's neck and withers, working my way slow and easy along his back and under his belly and across his wide rump.

It was hot, dusty work and I got dragged all over the corral but I had taken Contway's word that Moss Agate would be in my string next year and that was all that mattered.

The two bronc tamers were in the big corral working with the other colts. I was left alone and that was how I wanted it. When the colt wiped his sweaty head on me,

I was about as happy as a kid could be. Even at the start, before he came anywhere near getting used to me, there was no white showing when he rolled his dark brown, almost velvet black eye to watch what I was doing.

I knew I could put my trust in a horse with eyes like that, once he got used to my smell and the sound of my voice. Contway had told me that a kid could do more with a green colt than a man, if the kid didn't lose his temper, and I sure wasn't letting mine slip a notch.

I had Moss Agate to where I could slap the blanket all over him and he never even flinched. The sacking-out job was about finished around four in the afternoon when Contway lugged his saddle into the corral.

I shook the dust from the old saddle blanket and put it on Moss Agate's back. When Contway eased on the saddle I went around to the off side to straighten the cinch and pass it under the colt's belly. He humped his back a little when the cinch tightened, but that was all.

We let the colt wear the saddle. He crowhopped when I led him and I had to step lively to keep out of the way. I kept a grip on the rope and led him around saddled till I got leg weary, then I tied the rope to the saddle strings and let him "salt" for a while.

When Contway eased himself into the saddle later on, Moss Agate bucked a few jumps, but in the small round corral he couldn't do much bucking, and in no time the grizzled half-breed had him trotting around the corral.

When he'd gone around a couple of times Contway plow-reined him and let him travel in the other direction, then across the corral, back and forth, a dozen or twenty times. Then he got off and lead the colt, climbed back on, dismounted, and got back on until the colt would stand tracked.

"Fetch your saddle," Contway told me as he loosened his latigo.

I unsaddled Snowflake and lugged my saddle in. Contway sat in the shade smoking while I put on my saddle and tightened the cinch. Then he led in a gentle horse he used and saddled him and mounted. He snubbed the colt up close to his saddle horn, then pulled me up behind him. My legs were too short to mount the green colt, so I mounted him as he came alongside. I was tight inside and my knees were shaking, but I got over the nervousness by the time we went around a few times.

Charlie Brewster opened the gate that led into the big corral and we rode around that a dozen times, with Moss Agate cold snubbed to Contway's saddle horn on a slack ten-foot length of rope, enough so that I could plow-rein the colt, but if he got rank, his head could be jerked up.

I was just getting used to the feel of it when we went back into the small corral and Contway said to get off. The colt had learned enough for one day.

While I unsaddled, Contway and Brewster led the four colts they had tied up down to the barn. I rubbed the sweat off Moss Agate with the blanket and watered him from the tin bucket that held our drinking water. I got a dipperful first and rinsed out my mouth and drank the rest.

Snowflake was saddled by the time Contway came back. He turned the loose broncs into the pasture and led Moss Agate to the barn.

I'd be helping Contway and Brewster again tomorrow at the bronco breaking corrals.

I was dusty from head to foot, sweaty and tired and lame, skinned up and bruised in a few places from being dragged around the corral. I peeled off my clothes in the cabin and went for a swim in Beaver Creek that ran behind the ranch buildings.

I got into clean clothes as the supper bell rang. I was sure excited about having ridden my first bronc and I don't remember what I ate for supper that night, but whatever it was I finished in a hurry. All I wanted was to get back to the barn where Moss Agate was tied in the large double stall with Snowflake.

I was a little worried about how they would get along. Snowflake was so darned fussy about throwing in with any other horse. But when I got there they were both eating their heads off, so I kept out of the stall and sat down near the grain box to see how they made out.

I had no intention of dozing off, but it was dark when I came awake and for a second or so I didn't know where I was. But there was enough light in the barn to see Snowflake standing hipshot, asleep on his feet, and Moss Agate bedded down in the stall. I slipped out as quietly as I could and headed for my cabin.

Horace Brewster was coming out of the bunkhouse. "I hear you rode a bronc," he said.

Before I could ask how he knew, he said, "Your father was watching you for the best part of the afternoon, off and on, sittin' out near the brandin' chute."

"If I'd known he was watching. . . ."

"That's the reason he didn't show himself," Brewster smiled. Then he told me that my father said I was to have Moss Agate in my string next year. "By the time Joe Contway gets through with the colt this fall, you'll have a cow horse you can brag about next roundup," Brewster said.

I went to sleep with a grin on my face that night. I rode my first bronc and my father had claimed him for me.

CHAPTER SIX

The Harness Race

The annual harness race, matched between my father's team and the teams of my brothers Bob and Will and Wallace, between the home ranch and the cow town of Malta, had been a tradition as far back as I could remember.

Each one of them would put up a thousand dollars, winner take all. And every man on the ranch and the town citizens had bet money that ran into a considerable amount.

That yearly harness race at the Circle C had become a sort of celebration that called for a holiday.

I was in the office the night before when my father and Bob and Will made their bets. Wallace was in Helena and his team was out of the race this year. This was the first time my father had taken me.

I looked the horses over while I grained them in their stalls. There was little difference in their breeding and conformation. The Tucker bays, Bob's Lewis and Clark bald-faced, stocking-legged chestnuts, Will's seal-brown Roulette and Faro. Every horse was sound as a dollar, sleek and beautiful, without a blemish, each conditioned for the long, gruelling, forty-five mile road race.

Father's new top buggy had arrived a few days ago. It had been made to order by an Eastern firm, with every

64

piece of wood carefully selected. The top and dashboard were of solid leather the color of gun metal, a special leather that wouldn't crack as it weathered. The tires were hard rubber instead of iron, and the hardwood wheels varnished to bring out the grain.

I remembered something Old Tom had told me when he worked on Big Ned's feet; that a lot of horse races had been won or lost according to the condition of a horse's hoofs. So I went into the stall with Nip and Tuck, and lifting each hoof between my knees, I cleaned out the dirt and manure with a hoof pick. "Don't give us any alibis about pulling up lame," I told the Tucker bays as I slapped them on the rumps.

I knew if my father had seen me he would have ordered me out of the stall, but I'd been making up to Nip and Tuck when nobody had been around.

Frank Howe and Joe Contway helped Will and Bob hook their teams to the buggies. Humpy Jack Davis and Pete Olsen held the horses' heads till Bob and Will got into the rigs.

Brewster and I held the Tucker bays while father climbed into the buggy seat and got a grip on the reins. Then I let go of Nip's bridle and scrambled over the front wheel into the seat beside my father.

Every man on the ranch was there to watch the start. When the three buggies were lined up, my father called out in a loud voice, "Turn loose! Let's go!"

We were off in a cloud of dust, the three rigs all but hub to hub for a short distance. Then father let Bob and Will pull ahead to fight it out between them to see who

65

would get to the one-way road first. It was like a three team runaway for a short while, every man for himself, and all were out for blood.

Bob cut in on two wheels and got the road by a narrow margin, almost piling the two buggies in a bad wreck. By the time we crossed Little Warm bridge, five miles from the starting line, the Tucker bays were a half mile behind in the dust.

"It's the last five miles that count," my father chuckled as he held his team down to a steady road trot.

It had been trying to rain for two weeks or more. The late July night had been sultry, and now the black thunderheads piled up behind the twin buttes were rumbling and sheet lightning smeared the heavy sky behind the Little Rockies.

We were nearing the halfway station called the Hog Ranch, when the storm hit. The whole sky, that had hung low overhead like an enormous black sack filled with water, let out a Noah's Ark flood. One minute the road ahead was filled with heavy dust, a minute later the deep wagon ruts were running muddy water. For a while we had to squint our eyes half shut to see the ears of the team as the wind whipped the rain against us.

My father wore a pair of new overalls over his suit pants to keep the dust off. I knew they would look like they had been left overnight in a tub of blueing when the dye ran. His white mustache and beard were wet, and before long he would look like the well digger McGinty after he had just climbed up the well rope. I was getting plenty damp myself.

66

The low sod-roofed log buildings of the Hog Ranch stage station loomed up ahead. Beyond Hog Ranch lay a mile or more of road known as the Red Lane, because of its red gumbo clay. In rainy weather it was the boggiest strip of road that ever mired a wagon to the hubs.

Charlie Whitcomb, a mining man and close friend of the family, was standing in the saloon dooorway as we drove past to the log barn.

"Jump out and tie up the horses' tails," father told me. "And step lively."

I jumped out and with the help of the stock tender, who came out of the barn to lend a hand, we braided each tail in three plaits, then twisted the braid up and around and knotted it above the hocks so it couldn't come loose. It was a makeshift job but it would do to keep the long tails from balling up with sticky gumbo.

Whitcomb came over wearing a slicker, which he took off and made my father put on. He took a silver-cased stop watch from his vest pocket and said, "Bob's seven minutes and twenty seconds in the lead. You're five minutes and forty-two seconds behind Will."

"You got any money down, Charlie?" father asked.

"Five hundred on Bob," Whitcomb grinned, then said, "That cloudburst caught Bob's rig at the far end of the Red Lane ahead. Will's team was caught in the broad middle, far enough in so he couldn't turn around, and they're sloggin' through the gumbo hock deep." Whitcomb shrugged his bulky shoulders and made a sort of hopeless gesture with his hands.

"With a mile of red gumbo churned up like it is, you'll

bog that bay team down to the ears. That cloudburst throwed you the race, Mr. Coburn. From the Red Lane to Malta it'll be a matched race between Bob and Will, if Will gets through."

"Wipe the grin off your face, Whitcomb," father snapped. "I got five hundred that says the Tucker bays get my rig to Malta in the lead. Money talks the only language in a hoss race," he snapped, blue sparks glinting in his eyes.

I gave the tied-up tails a final yank to make sure they were tight and scrambled back into the buggy as father backed the team.

"It's a bet!" Whitcomb called out as the front wheels cramped in a tight turn.

The rain had let up enough to see the length of muddy red gumbo road ahead, the ditches on each side filled with water. A rig had to stay in the ruts or tip over into six feet of water. With Will's rig crawling the ruts ahead it seemed worse than hopeless for us to tackle it. The rain closed in like a gray blanket now.

Without saying a word, my father swung Nip and Tuck off the road just before we reached the Red Lane, and headed across country, twisting between clumps of brush. I got busy and buckled down the side curtains.

"Five miles," my father said as if talking to himself. "About five miles around. We'll give them that for boot. Hit the gravel crossing on Wild Horse Creek. It'll be touch and go. Wild Horse will flood its banks directly and we got to race against time." The buggy whip hissed a foot or so above the team and they lengthened out, the rig bouncing.

"Take a look in the jockey box," my father told me. "See what's there that can be used to cut a wire fence."

I found an old pair of long-handled nippers used to trim horses' hoofs, and when we came to B. D. Phillips sheep fence near the crossing on Wild Horse, I jumped out and cut the wire close to the posts. It was a five-strand fence of twisted barbwire and it took all my strength to do the cutting.

When I climbed back in, my father had taken off his slicker. He told me to roll up the side curtains.

He pulled up at the edge of a thirty-foot stretch of muddy water running bank to bank, and I walked out along the wagon tongue to release the check reins, talking to Nip and Tuck as I crept forward, a hand on each horse's back.

Swimming a stream in a top buggy was a new experience for me. I learned to swim the Missouri River when I was so high and I had no fear for myself. But I was afraid for my father, for I knew he couldn't swim a stroke.

"Stay on your side of the seat," father instructed me. "Hang onto the side brace. The buggy will tip sideways when we reach swimming water, so lean out as far as you can. If we turn over, let go and strike out for shore. You'll be on your own. I'll have my hands full with the team."

I looked at him and asked, "Can you swim?"

"You don't need to swim if you know how to handle a team in water," he said. He brought the whip down across the rumps of both horses' standing stiff-legged, reluctant to take to the swift running water. Now they snorted and hit the collars and lunged belly deep.

The current hit the buggy broadside, tipping it slowly.

I hung on and swung out as I had been told. My father slid his weight on the tilted seat to the upstream side and the buggy came back slowly on even keel. He began talking to the horses who were swimming hard, snorting as if they had rollers in their nostrils. "Steady . . . steady now . . . steady boys. . . ." There was no fear in his calm, even-toned voice as he handled the reins gently, knowing that a horse will come over backwards in swimming water if there is any hard pull on his mouth.

A few minutes later the horses struck gravel and dug in, hauling the buggy up the slant of the far bank. When the rig was on solid ground, we pulled up, to wind the horses.

I walked out on the tongue again to fasten the check reins while father was making up his mind whether to go back to the road or cut across country some more.

"We'll head straight across," he made his decision aloud. And we were off again, bouncing over brush and boulders, down cutbanks and up slants.

We were a good fifteen miles or more from Malta and we had gone five miles out of our way. That five miles had used up time, but we were still in the race.

The rain had cooled out the grain-fed bays and in spite of the heavy going, they reached out for all they had when we got back on the road.

I kept watching ahead to catch sight of the other two rigs, but after an hour and no sign of them I started getting worried. By the time we reached West Alkali bridge I gave up all hope of overtaking them. I began to feel the chill of my wet clothes and my teeth were chattering. I could tell my father was bone cold by the pinched look on his face, but he never let on.

We were within five miles of Malta when we sighted a rig ahead. "There's one of 'em," I shouted. "Half a mile ahead."

"We'll take care of that half mile, directly." My father clucked at the team and shook out the lines a little and the bays lengthened their stride. "It ain't time to ask 'em yet," he said. "Watch their tails."

There was a two mile stretch of road across a wide flat strip of benchland. I watched the tied-up tails that father said were sure indicators of whatever reserve strength was left in a horse on a gruelling trip. If the tails had been tied to short broomsticks they couldn't have been straighter.

The Tucker bays sighted the rig ahead as quickly as we had. I swear those two horses looked at each other and swapped a couple of words of horse talk, because they let out another notch of their own accord. I heard my father chuckle as he looked to see if I'd noticed. I tried to get a grin on my face, but if it was as mud-spattered as his, it must have looked like a cracked mud pie.

The buggy ahead was Will's. As we came up even I saw the red smear in his thick black hair and the blood on his face. One side of the buggy looked caved in, both side curtains had been ripped off, and a ragged hole showed in the patent leather top. Roulette and Faro's brown coats were mud spattered, the buggy plastered with sticky gumbo, and Will looked like he had taken a mud bath.

"Schoolhouse Coulee bridge washed out from under me!" he yelled as he reined off the road to let us pass.

71

"Bob's somewhere ahead! Pass him and I'll buy you a chicken dinner!" He waved the buggy whip in salute as we showered him with muddy water from a big puddle in the middle of the road.

As we rounded a bend in the road within a mile of town we sighted Bob's rig. We had a fifty yard gap to close and button up fast. My father reached for the whip.

"Hah! Hah! Hah!" The short words barked at the team with a startling sound like dry sticks snapping. It was as if he had jabbed them with a prod pole.

Bob couldn't see us coming because his rear window was mud-plastered and he was too busy getting the last licks out of Lewis and Clark.

There was a straightway hundred yards of sagebrush flat ahead and beyond that two pasture fences made a narrow lane. We had to beat Bob to the lane, so father quit the road and took to the brush.

"Hah! Hah!" The Tucker bays reached out, the buggy bouncing and jolting on three wheels, tipping sideways with two wheels spinning in the air, then bouncing back on all four wheels.

The two teams were neck and neck with Bob not giving an inch of the muddy road as he laid the whip across the rumps of the mud-covered chestnut team.

"Make your bid," father's voice sounded in my ear. "Ask 'em! Ask 'em!"

"Nip!" I hollered. "Tuck! Pick 'em up!" I let out an Indian yip and almost bit off my tongue as the rig bounced over a clump of brush. We were past Bob's rig and coming to the narrow lane. I cut a quick look back as father reined onto the road and saw Bob pull on the lines to keep from piling up. In the distance Will's rig seemed to be gaining ground fast.

Nip and Tuck were wide open now. The rear wheel on my side grazed the corner post as we passed into the lane.

A quarter mile ahead was the cow town of Malta. Two rain-washed, red brick, two-story buildings loomed up. They were the Great Northern Hotel and Trafton's Store that marked the finish line. The wide dirt street was a mud puddle lake.

It was that last quarter mile, the final lap of the grueling forty-five miles harness race, that would tell the tale. The only difference between the three buggy teams, almost identical in conformation, with equal breeding and pedigreed bloodline, was the proverbial difference of opinion that makes for a matched race.

Will's Roulette and Faro had crept up on Bob's Lewis and Clark sorrels. Father's Tucker bays were no more than a buggy length ahead when we came into the homestretch. It was still any man's race, and this was the supreme test of game-hearted horses and skilled drivers.

The three rigs hit that last hundred yard stretch of muddy water wide open.

It looked like every man in Malta was in the milling crowd that shoved and elbowed on the wide plank walks on either side of the street, heedless of the drizzle. Every man must have had a bet down the way they hollered and yelled at the tops of their lungs, to bring in the team they bet on. The roar of the milling crowd swelled up and came at us like rolling thunder.

The westbound had just pulled in at the crossing. The train crew must have seen what was going on, for the wail of the locomotive whistle and the clang of the engine bell added to the din.

The three rigs were abreast now, almost hub to hub on the wide street; less than a hundred yards to go. Mud chunks and water sprayed out on all sides. The mud coating made the horses all one color. The buggies and drivers were mud-splattered. Horses and rigs and men lost identity.

This was it; the final test.

My father's loud shout lifted above the confusion of noise. "Hah! Hah! Hah!" The long black buggy whip whistled a warning a foot above the wet backs of the team, back and forth, back and forth, as it slashed the drizzle, the water almost hub deep.

The Tucker bays reached out, every muscle, every tendon strained to the utmost, giving the last of the strength that was rock bottom reserve, racing their hearts out.

I was crouched down on the carpeted floor, holding onto the dashboard and leaning out, blinded by the mud splashing into my face. I was hollering, calling to the two horses, yelling at them to git, git, git! I was so close I could reach out and almost touch Nip's rump, calling to them for the last bid, half sobbing and bawling with strong emotion.

The wild cheering roar of the crowd closed in from all sides, heedless of the mud and water that drenched them.

I knuckled the mud out of my eyes with one hand and looked around. Bob's team was a length away, almost scraping hubs with Will's rig. It was a race between the two teams for second place. I was reminded of the chariot race in *Ben Hur.*

The Tucker bays were a buggy length ahead when we crossed the finish line. B. D. Phillips, standing on a chair, was waving his hat, letting out a war whoop, yelling like an Assiniboin. He had a stop watch in his hand as we finished a daylight length ahead.

I grabbed Nip's tail that had come undone, pulled it over the dashboard, and hung on. Out of the corner of my eye I saw father lift his whip in a salute as we crossed the finish line.

"You did fine, son," father's unsteady voice sounded a long way off in my mud-plastered ears. "Get back up on the seat and take the lines."

Never, if I live to be as old as Methuselah, will that moment ever come again. A horseman's victory, shared by as fine a span of horses as ever gave the best that was in the heart of a thoroughbred. And when father put the lines into my muddied hands, entrusting the Tucker bays into my care, he gave me something that was beyond value. He passed on his horsemanship and love for a horse to me as a legacy. Knowing that somehow I had earned it made me feel both humble and proud. It gave me an understanding of my parent that I had never before felt.

I walked the team to the livery barn. I unhooked the muddy traces from the singletree and unbuckled the neck yoke straps and hung collars and harness on wooden pegs. Then I led them around by halter ropes for a half hour until they were cooled out. After that I watered them slowly and filled their feed boxes with oats, and forked timothy and bluejoint into the mangers. While they ate I went to work with currycomb and brush and when I finished, their mahogany bay coats shone like polish on a gambler's shoes.

While Nip and Tuck stood hock deep in fresh straw bedding, I rubbed their legs with strong-smelling horse liniment until the quart bottle was empty and my fingers were cramped.

Long after the barn man had finished caring for Lewis and Clark and Roulette and Faro, I was there telling the Tucker bays about how they had won the race. It was strictly horse talk, not meant for human ears.

I hadn't meant to spend the whole afternoon there but I did. I was still there when my father finally located me. He said he had been hunting all over town for me. He looked at his watch and it was almost six o'clock. He said if I was to get outfitted from the skin out at the Mercantile, and get a hot bath and haircut at Shorty's Barber Shop, I'd better shake a leg. He handed me a ten-dollar bill and said we'd eat that chicken dinner on Will at the Great Northern Hotel.

He looked the bay team over. "Slick as seals," he said as we walked out of the barn, his arm across my shoulder. "You did a first-rate job on that team, son. Old Tom couldn't have done better." He asked me if I had taken a look at the other two teams.

I told him I saw to it that the horses were cooled out before they were watered and grained, had fresh hay in their managers, and clean straw bedding. I reminded him of what he'd always told me—never leave it to a livery

76

stable hired hand to take care of a horse. Those two teams belonged to the ranch, and it was my job.

An hour later I came out of Shorty's Barber Shop in my town clothes. I'd had a bath and a haircut.

After dinner at the hotel with father and my brothers, I walked down the street feeling warm and good inside. I didn't know a kid in town my age so I was going on a high lonesome. I had money in my pocket and there was nothing to stop me from painting the town a strawberry-pop red.

As I walked along whistling through my teeth I kept thinking of the play I had seen at the Great Falls Opera House—Dustin Farnum in *The Virginian*. I'd read the book twice and to my way of thinking the outlaw Trampas was the hero. And the Virginian had no business turning traitor to the cowpuncher who had been his friend. I likened Trampas to Kid Curry, and the Kid was my friend, and I felt I sort of belonged to the Wild Bunch.

I remembered the song that Trampas sang and I started humming it as I headed across the tracks for Doc Murray's Drug Store for a soda pop and some ice cream and candy.

> "Ten thousand cattle straying. . . .
> I quit my range and traveled away,
> So it's sons a guns,
> That's what I say!
> I've gambled my money
> All away!"

I was Trampas in my black sateen shirt as I walked along with my new Stetson at an angle across my eyes.

CHAPTER SEVEN

I Meet the Governor of Montana

One morning the end of August my father took me to the top of the east butte of the twin Coburn Buttes. It was one of those clear cloudless Montana days when you could see for forty miles with the naked eye.

When we reached the top that was covered with scrub pine my father swung down and loosened his saddle cinch and let his horse blow. I was riding Snowflake and I knew enough to do likewise.

I remember how my father stood there for a long time, his small shaped Stetson hat pulled down to shade his puckered eyes that were the color of a rain-washed Montana sky. Finally he made a wide gesture with his arm, pointing toward the north and slowly swinging to the east and to the south and then to the west.

"That's Circle C range," he said quietly, pride in the tone of his voice, "as far as the eye can see in all directions. Part of it's yours, son. See that you take care of your interest."

"Yes, sir," I answered as I looked out toward the distant sky line.

If he had been a man given to making speeches, he could have told me how he had built up the outfit. How he had come to Montana Territory in '63, and how his isolated ranch, then on Flatwillow, had been surrounded by Chief Joseph and his Nez Percés, who were on the warpath, pursued by General Miles and his cavalry. He could have told me about the early morning he had walked out alone to meet Chief Joseph and exchange gifts and smoke, while his wife and two small children were inside the house with his one cow hand, Horace Brewster. He had given Brewster instructions to shoot his family rather than let them fall into the hands of the Indians.

The long-stemmed peace pipe carved from red pipestone that Chief Joseph and my father had smoked was in our house in Great Falls, together with an elk-tooth necklace and a war bonnet made of dyed horsehair. In exchange for those gifts my father had given the Indian Chief a beef steer to butcher for his hungry war party.

My father, one of the Vigilantes of Montana Territory, could have told me stories of the hangings of the road agents and horse thieves and cattle rustlers in the Judith Basin country. He could have related the story of the hard winter of '86–'87 that had wiped out the cattlemen, and about those who survived having to start again from scratch.

But he told me nothing of these things. Perhaps he was thinking of it all as he looked out across the country and back across the years. Somehow, young as I was, I halfway understood.

This morning on top of East Butte he had taken me along for one purpose, to put a man's burden on my kid shoulders.

When he tightened the cinch on his big brown gelding,

Reader, I knew it was time to go. I tightened my saddle cinch by putting the latigo strap across my shoulder and pulling, then knotting it through the ring of my small single-rigged, center-fire saddle, using a four-in-hand knot. Maneuvering the little cow pony alongside a big boulder, I climbed on before he could step away.

On the way back down the sloping butte a black diamond rattlesnake, coiled on the rocky trail ahead, sounded its warning. My father got off his horse with his rawhide quirt looped on his wrist. When the rattler struck, falling short of its target, the quirt lashed out at the flat head. A couple more quirts at the head and then he stomped it into the hard ground with his boot heel. He cut off the rattles and handed them to me. I counted fourteen and what is known as the button, the new black rattle next to the tail. I put the rattles in my hatband.

On the way back to the ranch we rode through a couple hundred head of grazing cattle, a mixed bunch of cows and calves and steers. As we rode through my father would point out a steer and ask me its age; yearling, two-year-old, three-year-old or a four-year-old ready for the fall market? It was hard to judge the age from a two-year-old on. I didn't do so well and he finally gave up.

I did better when I read him the brands and earmarks on the strays in the bunch; brands like the Circle Diamond and Long X and Long S, the Milner Square, the Mill Iron, the I.D.

The Bar L and Four T and Rafter T belonged to our outfit, along with the Half-Circle C. These brands were easy and I made no mistakes.

Reading earmarks was something else, especially on the cows and big steers with the long hair in the ears to add to the difficulty. On a freshly marked calf it was simple enough to tell the mark: Crop, Underbit and Overbit, Underslope and Overslope, Swallowfork, Slit. But these were grown cattle and the earmarks haired-over and I got to where I was guessing on half the marks.

"I hope you do better next year," was all my father said when he finally headed for the ranch at a jog trot, the range gait of a cowpuncher ahorseback.

I had learned at the beginning never to expect any praise for a job well done. If it was done right, that was all in a day's work, an ordinary thing. Cow hands didn't expect or get praised for doing a job well, no matter how difficult or dangerous that chore was in the sixteen-hour average day of a working cow hand. And I was learning the cow business.

Reader had a slow trot that ate up the miles. My shorter legged Snowflake pony traveled at a high trot to keep up. I was wishing either Reader would break into a lope or slow down to a walk, but he didn't.

My father must have had his mind on something else because he seemed to have forgotten that I was along. But I knew what would happen if I dropped behind. He'd make his usual remark, "Whip up. Don't trail behind like an Injun." I knew what he meant. White men rode alongside each other; Indians rode single file.

I started to get a sideache. It felt like a dull knife twisting with each trotting step. I had seen lots of cowpunchers ride standing in the stirrups, one hand on the saddle horn.

I tried it now, but my legs were too short. We had about two miles to go and all I could do was grit my teeth and sweat it out.

It was then that Horace Brewster came riding out of a long draw about a quarter mile away. My father slowed down to a walk to let him overhaul us. No horsebacker ever made a more welcome sight.

He had been in Malta for the past few days to see about ordering cattle cars for the first beef shipment over the Great Northern Railway. I heard him tell my father, "The best I could do was the seventh."

Brewster showed up in the nick of time before I keeled over. But he sure carried bad news for me. He had promised to take me on the fall roundup, due to start tomorrow or the next day, and he had figured on shipping about September first. That would have given me two weeks with the roundup before I had to leave for school which started the day after Labor Day, on the third. Much as my father wanted me to learn the cow business, schooling came first with him, and I knew I would be in Great Falls the day school started, regardless.

I had to fight back the tears of disappointment as I lagged behind. When the roundup started I would be at the ranch with a bunch of hay hands or on my way to Great Falls two weeks before schooltime. My heart was set on going on the beef roundup and Brewster had promised he would order the cattle cars and ship out on the first. But he must have forgotten about me.

My father and Brewster had unsaddled when I got to the barn. The noon dinner bell rang and everybody quit work and headed for the bunkhouse to wash up and eat. I stayed to water whatever horses were in the barn, that being my chore.

I was half sick with worry and disappointment about the bad news Brewster had fetched, but I wouldn't say anything about my troubles to any of the cowpunchers. There was nothing they could do about it, and I didn't want any sympathetic talk about it being my hard luck.

I led Reader and Snowflake to the water trough and dropped the halter ropes. Something had gone wrong with the windmill and the trough was almost empty. I filled the lard pail used to prime the pump from water in the trough and started pumping, swinging my weight on the pump handle. Filling a thirty foot long horse trough by hand is a job for a man. For a pint-sized kid it was twice as hard and took a long time.

I was puffing and sweating and my arms and shoulders and back were aching. And as if I didn't have troubles enough, those darned horses started teasing each other, their ears laid back and teeth bared. Reader and Snowflake were side pardners and it was all in fun, but they got to pawing the trough and Reader got a foreleg over the side and commenced splashing and, of course, Snowflake had to do the same.

I had been careless about wrapping the two halter ropes around one of the poles of the fence that went around the well and pump, and now they were loose and wet and were being tromped in the mud around the trough. I knew the trough had to be filled and I made up my mule-headed hind I wasn't going to let that pair of clown horses get me away from swinging on the pump handle.

My back was toward the trough and I was blowing hard when I heard a man's voice behind me. "Here's another horse to water, boy. And you might as well unsaddle the nag and put him in the barn. I won't be needing him this afternoon."

I let go the pump handle and straightened my back to get the kinks out, and looked around. It was one of the pair of city dudes from Helena who were spending the week end at Bob's house. One of them was the President of the National Bank, a big, paunchy man named Alex Johnson. This man was the one he'd brought along. He was tall with gray hair and mustache, and wore old corduroy pants and a canvas hunting coat. The large game pockets were bulging with young prairie chicken he had shot. When he swung down from the saddle, he lifted his shotgun across his shoulder and started to walk away.

I had saddled a gentle horse for him that morning and left it tied in the barn, a blazed-face old gentle bay gelding that Wallace had gun broke. Anyone could shoot off his back. Old Snipe's hide showed the salt white sweat marks from carrying the big city dude all morning. He had his face in the trough drinking. That dude didn't even have sense enough to take the headstall off, and the old cavalry bit kept hanging up on the edge of the trough.

Somehow that was the last straw on the camel's back, coming like it did on top of my other troubles. I'll never know what made me talk up like I did to an older man that I knew was Bob's guest, but I just couldn't help myself.

"I was brought up," I told him sharply, "to always take care of the horse that packed me before I took care of myself."

I was so mad that my voice trembled. I must have looked silly with my dirty face and the sweat trickling down, sounding off like that.

I saw him take notice of me for the first time, then his eyes sort of puckered at the corners and he grinned. The grin made me mad.

"Old Snipe can't drink good with that long shanked bit in his mouth. Besides you got the cinch pulled up till he's cut in two." I knew I'd said too much, but it was too late to take anything back.

The best thing for me to do was to go back to the pump handle, and that's what I did.

"A man can live too long in the city," I heard him say. Out of the corner of my eye I watched him slip the headstall off and release the cavalry bit. Then he slacked the tight latigo.

When Old Snipe had his fill, the man led him to the barn and skinned off the saddle. He was forking hay from the loft into the manger when I led Reader and Snowflake in and tied them in their stalls. I took my time till he went out.

When I came out of the barn I saw him working the pump handle. It looked like he was pitching in, lending me a hand, when I led his livery team out to water. He grinned at me. He had shed his coat.

I saw my father coming. He and the man working the pump handle smiled at each other.

"Working up an appetite, Governor?" my father called out.

"That too, Mister Coburn," he chuckled, "I've just been put in my proper place. For having been raised on a farm, I had forgotten certain things I should have remembered."

The trough was filled and overflowing. The man held the big tin dipper under the spout until it was full of water, then he drained it and hung it back on the nail. Next he picked up his hunting coat with the mess of young prairie chicken in the pockets.

"Son," my father said to me, "wipe the dirt off and shake hands with the Governor of Montana."

If ever I wanted to dig a hole and pull it in on top of me, this was it. I felt the cold sweat pop out.

"We've already met," the Governor said, winking at me behind my father's back. Then he reached out and gripped my hand and somehow I knew everything was all right when he put his hand on my shoulder.

But all the same I was plenty relieved when the horses quit drinking and I could lead them back to the barn.

"That boy of yours gave me something I'm going to fit into my next stump speech when I'm campaigning the cow towns," I heard the Governor tell my father. "A man who can't take care of his horse is not deserving of the good will of the cow country. That's one for the book," he chuckled.

I sure hoped he wasn't going to tell it for a joke on himself to my father or Bob, because they wouldn't get a laugh out of it. I had run off at the mouth like a smart-alecky kid who wasn't dry behind the ears, and he was the Governor of Montana and a ranch guest! I'd be lucky if I wasn't on tomorrow's stage, headed for Great Falls.

After dinner I was on my way to the log cabin where I slept. I had to pass the office and I overheard Brewster say, "I promised the boy I'd take him on the roundup. Missin' a week's school won't do no harm."

"Quit spoilin' the kid," Bob put in. Then my father settled the argument I knew they were having about me going on the roundup. "The boy starts school when he's supposed to, Brewster. You're too free with your promises."

I had heard all I needed to know. Brewster had done his best but he was outvoted three to one. I stumbled to my cabin, half blinded with tears and disappointment, to pack my clothes.

When I went in, Bridget, the big wolfhound, had her litter of pups on one of the two bunks. We had bred her to Don, the big Airedale that Teddy Roosevelt had sent Wallace for a bear dog. Bridget was stretched out, letting the pups get their dinner.

When the pups saw me they quit nursing and swarmed all over me. I had to get down on all fours and play with them. Dog fleas never bothered me or Wallace like they did Will and Bob and my father, who wouldn't set foot inside the log cabin.

The pups had me down, growling and chewing on my clothes when Brewster opened the door and looked in. He had a pasteboard box that had just come in the mail. He handed it to me, and when I read the label, C. H. Hyer & Sons, Olathe, Kansas, I knew my new boots had arrived.

Brewster chuckled and said, "Your chances of goin' on

the roundup were plumb gone, until the Governor took your part and your father agreed to let you come along." I could hardly believe my ears.

I guess that was the happiest moment I had ever had. My hands shook as I unwrapped the shiny black boots, with colored stitching on the tops. I pulled off my old scuffed shoes and got a clean pair of sox from my warsack. I sat on the edge of the bunk and pulled the boots on and tried to thank Brewster the best way I knew how.

"Better take them off and hide them till we start on the roundup," he said. "If Will or Bob see the boots they'd chaw me out. They say I'm spoilin' you."

I wrapped the boots in the tissue and put them in my warsack. I went around doing my chores that evening in a sort of daze.

After supper I was in the bunkhouse with the cowpunchers when Humpy Jack dug from his bedroll a pair of secondhand chaps with short curly black hair, and tossed them at me. He had cut the legs down and shortened the belt to fit me, explaining that it might turn cold, and when a man's legs were cold he was cold all over.

I came in for some rough joshing and ribbing from the cowpunchers who liked to tease and plague a kid. I had a quick temper and they liked to get me riled up to where I'd cuss and bawl. But whenever the joshing got too rough, the nighthawk would step in and take it up. Humpy Jack had a waspish temper and a colorful vocabulary of cuss words of his own coinage. In a ruckus he was hard to whip. When he was in good humor his high-pitched rasping laugh could be heard for a mile.

When bedtime came I shut the log cabin door and lit the candle. I put on my new boots and the chaps and admired myself, tilting the cracked shaving mirror, with its slightly wavy glass, so the reflection showed the boots and chaps. Finally, I took off the chaps but I slept that night with my boots on.

Next morning, before daylight, I had to use the boot-jack to pry off the shopmade, tight-fitting boots. I put my shoes on and took the chaps to the barn to keep Bridget's pups from tearing them apart.

After breakfast, preparations for the roundup were underway.

The roundup cook and the bookkeeper were checking the grub list and loading the mess wagon. Blackstrap, the black tomcat, was curled up on the high seat. He was about ten years old and had not missed a spring or fall roundup since he had had his eyes open. He had been born in the mess box one summer between roundups and the mess wagon was his home.

The blacksmith shop was busy as a beehive. Baldy Clark, the smithy, and his helper were stripped to undershirts and each wore a leather shoeing apron over his pants. Baldy worked at the anvil shaping the red-hot shoes his helper took from the fire with a long-handled spike. When he had hammered a shoe into shape he took it outside and fitted it to the already trimmed hoof, a practiced eye the only gauge he needed.

Frank Howe and Fred Roberts, both good farriers, were doing the actual shoeing, trimming the hoofs with nippers and rasps and tacking on the shoes Baldy Clark dropped into a wooden tub of water to cool.

With skilled farriers like Howe and Roberts doing the shoeing, and an expert like Baldy Clark fitting the shoes, the job of shoeing the roundup horses went fast.

There was a great fascination to the blacksmith shop for me and it was there I stayed most of the morning. The ring of the smithy's hammer was music in my ears and the shower of white-hot sparks from the anvil was like shooting stars. The smell of the hot metal and the smoke from the soft coal, the hard packed dirt floor, horse and man sweat, and the odor of charred leather shoeing aprons, the blackened log walls, all seeped with old traditions that dated back across the generations.

To me it was a conjuring place, and the blacksmith had his own special niche in the frontier West, for without him the wagon trains were crippled. A brawny, lusty man with calloused hands, ribald, gentle around a horse; his shop, with its rows of horseshoes hung within easy reach of his anvil, was his primitive castle.

After noon dinner, I helped Humpy Jack put the double sideboards on the new Studebaker bed wagon, and fit the hardwood hoops that held the canvas top.

Later we stacked the branding irons in the inside rack of the end gate, the handles, fashioned to fit a man's gloved hand, sticking up. Baldy Buck had hammered out the irons that were shaped in half circles, quarter circles, straight bar irons. The L and V irons were the stamp irons with which a skilled cow hand could make any brand registered in the brand book.

90

The horse wrangler had spent the morning checking the rope corral which he had strung out on the ground. It was also his job to help the roundup cook check the mess wagon and see that it was in good shape, along with the water barrels that had to be checked for leaks before being loaded. There would be a few dry camps before the end of the roundup.

CHAPTER EIGHT

Remuda on the Loose

I was the first to show up at the barn the next morning. Brewster had told the boys in the bunkhouse the night before that the roundup would pull out sometime the next day, and I aimed to be on hand bright and early.

I had the horses all led out to water and back in the barn, and was in the loft shoveling hay down into the mangers when my father came in. He was waiting for me when I climbed down the ladder.

"Think you can catch up on your studies if you miss the first week at school, son?" he asked.

"Yes, sir."

"Then I think there's nothing stopping you from going on the roundup. You're old enough. Good time to prove that you can make a hand."

The thrill of his deciding to let me go was tempered down a little by the fact that this was to be a kind of test. I was old enough to know what would be expected of me.

I saw the twinkle in his eye as he took out his watch and looked at it in the lantern light. "You must have met yourself coming to the barn. It lacks fifteen minutes of being four in the morning," he said.

I heard him chuckling to himself as he headed for the

cook shack for his morning coffee. I was cleaning the stalls when the first of the cowpunchers showed up.

"Want us all to get fired?" they commenced horrawing me. "The Old Gent shore ate us out when he came into the bunkhouse."

"Saddle up that white pony and drift, button," another one suggested. "Get a job with some outfit that won't get you up in the middle of the night. Time you bowed your neck and quit."

Brewster came in while I was trying to grin it off.

"I let the horse wrangler go to town to have a tooth pulled," he told me. "You'll have to wrangle the horses till he gets back."

There were over 250 head of Circle C horses in the remuda. The ones inclined to stray off were called "bunch quitters" so a bell was strapped on the neck of each bunch quitter who had his own following of horses he tried to lead off.

A good horse wrangler or nighthawk, sitting on a high knoll where he could get a panoramic view of the scattered, grazing remuda, had an instinctive practiced ear for the horse bells, and when a bell horse started drifting down a hidden coulee or draw, the man on the knoll could hear the telltale bell and head the little bunch back.

Once in a while a smart bell horse who had learned to keep the bell from making much racket, slipped away and it would be a game between the bell horse and the man.

Horse wrangling was a job in itself. A good wrangler was valuable to an outfit. Let a bunch of half a dozen horses stray off and a cow hand or two had to be sent out horse hunting, which meant the roundup crew would be short-handed until the horses were found.

A roundup moved once a day as a rule, sometimes twice on the spring calf roundup, where there was no beef herd to hold and move slowly. If a roundup was held up one day to hunt horses, it threw the schedule behind and out-of-kilter. This was of vital importance on the beef roundup where the cattle cars were, of necessity, ordered a couple of weeks in advance. They were on the stockyards siding on the date ordered, with the switch engine and train crew, and if the cattle were delayed getting to the yards, the cow outfit paid a penalty to the railroad.

I had spent a couple of weeks at the horse camp on Big Warm with Humpy Jack Davis during the summer. I had the names of every horse in the remuda entered in my tally book, and Jack had told me how to identify each one. It was easy enough to remember a bald-faced horse by name, or one with a white stripe down the face, or a stocking-legged horse. The buckskins and the Apaloosas were easy to remember, as were the roans. But a lot of Circle C horses were solid colors and I had to study each one for individual traits and any slight difference in conformation.

Humpy Jack had taught me to study the shape of a horse's head, the high or low withers, the length of his back, the slope of his rump, the shape of his neck, and how he carried his head. It came in handy now as I sat perched on the pole corral gate.

The entire remuda was inside one corral. The other corral was empty. Most of the cowpunchers were sitting around on the fence, their ketch-ropes ready in their hands, their saddles outside the gate.

Brewster had a tally book in his hand in which were the names of each cowpuncher and his string of ten horses. It was a copy of the list he and Bob and Will had spent long hours working over the night before.

When Brewster called out a name, that cowpuncher got down and worked his way through the milling horses with his coiled rope in his hand. If the man was a new hand on the ranch, Brewster pointed out the horse he named.

Roping was a skilled art that came from long months and years of practice. Corral roping on foot was a special part of the art of handling a ketch-rope. No expert corral roper ever swung a loop over his head to get the horses spooked and milling. He stood with a smaller than average loop cocked.

There was just one overhand or underhand pitch of the loop when the singled-out horse got into an advantageous position. If the cowhand missed his second throw some expert corral roper did it for him. If the roper was an old hand at cowpunching he knew there was no stigma attached to his lack of skill in corral roping.

Some of the best-working cow hands on the range couldn't rope their own horse inside a corral. A whole lot of top cow hands let a good corral roper catch their horses. This was especially true on the roundup where the remuda was held enclosed by a one-rope corral. Let a sorry roper catch a bronc by mistake and have the bronc run on the rope, and the milling was apt to result in the corral going down and the horses spilling out at a run.

95

When a bronc was roped, two or three men would be right there to swing enough weight on the taut rope to pull the bronc around and hold him tracked while the bronc stomper riding the rough string eased down the rope and got the hackamore on.

A cow hand was supposed to remember each horse assigned to his string when he led the horse through the gate and turned him into the empty corral. He was supposed to know each horse by name and be able to pick out any of his string of ten from the big remuda in the rope corral before daylight the next morning. That feat of memory was a matter of pride to a good cow hand.

To a greenhorn or pilgrim, if he ever saw a rope corral full of horses before daybreak of a rainy morning on a roundup, it would seem impossible, but to the old-time cow hand there was nothing out of the ordinary in it. It was a part of his forty-a-month job and all in a day's work.

The powdery corral dust boiled up and settled on horses and men. It coated his hide and hair, clogged his nostrils and left a gritty taste in his mouth.

There was a pail of well water and a dipper just outside the cutting corral, with a coating of dusty scum on top, and while every man knew it was there, nobody took a drink, even though the roof of his mouth was coated and dry.

Old time cowpunchers were a boneheaded, prideful tribe. I have watched them get wet to the skin before any of them would reach for the rolled yellow slicker tied behind the saddle cantle. It was a disgrace to pack a lunch or a canteen of water on a long hard day's ride. You went empty bellied from daybreak breakfast till you ate sundown supper at ranch or cow camp. You watered your horse first if you came to a creek or water hole, and you ate at night only after you'd fed your horse and turned him loose to graze. Any man who fed or watered himself first before he took care of the horse that packed him didn't deserve to be called a cow hand. That was one of the unwritten laws of the cow country, and one of the first things I learned.

I was spitting dust by the time the last horse was led through the gate. The sun was noon high. Humpy Jack had roped out the bunch quitters and strapped bells around each horse's neck.

After he had gotten his string of horses, each cowhand saddled and rode off. Will and Bob and Brewster, sweaty and dirty, forked their horses and left. My father got down off the corral, and rode away on his saddled horse.

I climbed aboard Snowflake and opened the far gate to let the remuda drift out of the corral by themselves, remembering not to haze them out so they'd crowd and jam up in the gate, knock a hip down or get to kicking. I counted the bells as they went out.

I was looking down at the bucket of water with the dusty scum when Humpy Jack rode up. He told me to let the horses drift to the reservation fence. He said he had left a can of tomatoes in the creek and some grub in a sack under some brush to the right of the reservation gate for me.

I asked the nighthawk when he wanted the remuda back.

"Brewster's moving the wagons sometime this afternoon, on a shakedown move to see that nothing's been left behind," Humpy Jack said. "He'll camp the wagons this side of the gate. I'll see that your bed's loaded on my wagon. Right now I got your blankets spread out on the ground to air. Last spring that bed of yours shed a million fleas that found new homes in every bedroll in the bed wagon. The reps went back to their outfits spreading the news that the Circle C outfit was lousy as a sheep camp." He cackled as he rode away, carrying the water pail he'd emptied out, the long-handled tin dipper clattering in the bucket.

I found the can of tomatoes in the creek when I washed up. In the grab sack Humpy Jack had left a couple of beef-steak sandwiches and two doughnuts. I squatted in the shade of the high serviceberry bushes and ate my lunch. I washed out the sack and tied it on my saddle, then stretched out on the ground to take five. My eyes were closed before my head was on the ground.

I came awake with a start. I was on my feet and in the saddle and had that white pony of mine on a high lope before you could say jack-in-the-box. The remuda I was supposed to watch was scattered and spilled to Kingdom Come. I tried to keep a count on the bells as I rode a wide circle. My breath was coming in dry sobs.

What had seemed like level country now was filled with cut coulees and hidden pockets of high brush that could hide a dozen head of horses. The rolling prairie had turned into broken, brushy badlands while I was taking a cat nap.

It seemed like every rep string was long gone and vanished. When I cocked an eye at the sun it was halfway down in the sky. That meant the five I'd taken had been two to three hours.

I was dripping with sweat and there wasn't a dry hair on

Snowflake. I had the long blacksnake out and was trying to snap the wide buckskin popper like Humpy Jack had taught me, to stir the bushed-up horses out into the open. The long lash got wrapped around my neck, knocking off my hat. I let the hat lay and landmarked the place by a big chokescherry bush.

I jumped a little bunch of horses in a coulee. The belled bunch quitter and the six head wore the Circle Diamond brand. Three from that string were missing. I was panicky and bawling with shame and a futile sort of anger and frustration. I swung the blacksnake again and let it pop out ahead. The whiplash caught Snowflake across his fat rump. He laid back his furry ears and squealed and crowhopped a jump or two. I lost my right stirrup and grabbed the horn before I got bucked off, but somewhere behind me was the horse wrangler's blacksnake I let drop as I clawed for the nubbin'.

I had made mistakes before, but this was the granddaddy of all mistakes. I thought in those minutes of agonized self-torture that if Snowflake threw me and my foot hung in the stirrup and he came to the ranch with my dead body, it would be far better than the disgrace I faced.

The remuda was scattered a thousand miles in all directions and I was trapped helpless in the broad middle. The faint, faraway sound of horse bells came from all sides.

I pushed Snowflake to the limit. The pony was dripping sweat and blowing. He slowed down to a walk, then balked on me. I kicked and quirted him once and he laid his ears back and kicked up behind. When Snowflake made up his mind about anything there was nothing I could do to change it, so I sat my saddle, sweating and bawling, while Snowflake took his time getting his wind back.

The mocking jangle of horse bells, all jumbled together without direction, pounded my eardrums. I made up my mind I couldn't face it. I decided to ride back to the reservation gate, and once inside, head for the Indian camps. Jesse Iron Horn would hide me out in the Little Rockies. Jesse and I were side pardners. We often talked about running off. I would give Jesse the chance to prove what he had said.

I knew then that I had seen the home ranch for the last time. The thought of facing my father and Will and Bob and Brewster broke me out in a fresh panic. I kicked Snowflake but he was balked in his tracks like a mule.

I thought I heard the crack of a pistol. It came again. The jangle of horse bells sounded nearer, then I heard Humpy Jack cussing and his blacksnake popping. That was the shot I thought I'd heard. A big bunch of horses came at a run over a little rise ahead with Humpy Jack keeping them close bunched behind.

Snowflake nickered and hit a trot. I told the nighthawk I had gone to sleep and let the remuda get away, and I didn't have the guts to face it. He let on like he hadn't heard a word I said, nor noticed the dried tear marks on my flushed, dusty face. No kid ever had a more loyal friend than Humpy Jack Davis.

"There's one of them oozly birds somewhere," he said, peering into the brush. "I keep hearin' it whistle. Shoves its head in the ground like an ostrich and whistles through its tail feathers." He handed me my hat, then the horse wrangler's blacksnake I had borrowed.

"Snowflake musta turned outlaw," he grinned at me, his green eyes showing in the sun. "Bucked off your hat and made you drop your whip, but you stuck on like a bronc peeler. You'll be ridin' the rough string before long." He hoorawed me a little, then rode off whistling the same tuneless song as he headed for the ranch.

Every horse in the remuda was spread out and grazing as he rode away.

A little before sundown I sighted the roundup wagons coming from the ranch. Brewster and his cowpunchers were riding in the lead. Humpy Jack was perched on the high spring seat of the bed wagon, with the bedrolls and tents under the wide wooden hoops, the branding irons racked at the back; the big rope corral coiled and swinging from the high endgate; the forked corral staubs, brisket high to a horse, stacked beside the branding irons. He had the four-horse team in a lather and slowed down to a steady trot.

George L., the roundup cook, drove his four gentle horses hitched to the mess wagon. Blackstrap was perched on the high seat beside him, claws dug in, back arched and tail bushed, like a halloween cat.

Within a half hour from the time the wagons pulled in on the roundup crossing on Beaver Creek, the camp was made—mess tent and bed tent up and staked down; a fire going in the stove and supper started; the rope corral up; the bedrolls on the ground.

101

The horse wrangler showed up about the time I got the remuda in.

Brewster was checking everything, to make sure nothing had been left behind. Like other outfits our first day's move was only a short distance from the home ranch. It was a shakedown move to check and test the wagons and general equipment.

The wheels on both wagons were being rechecked to make doubly sure that the iron tires were firm and solid on the wooden rims and every wagon spoke set firm. The canvas covers were stretched over the wagon bows and tied down, to test them for holes. The wagons with the extra sideboards took on the appearance of prairie schooners. The bed tent was put up for the same reason and to make sure the poles were in good condition and the tent stakes all there. Leaky wagon sheets can do damage to beds and grub in the mess wagon. Leaky tents in bad weather make for bad-tempered cow hands.

Even the sheet-iron heating stove that went into the bed tent was set up and the stovepipe fitted. Before the beef roundup ended in late fall there would be cold rainy weather, perhaps a sleety drizzle that would end in a snowstorm. A cowpuncher, after a long cold wet day, wants a dry bed and a warm tent at night, hot grub and dry tobacco.

There was no beef herd to hold that night. No night guards to stand. The nighthawk was the only man who needed a horse.

Brewster roped a horse and saddled up and tied him to the bed wagon. He was riding back to the ranch after supper to have a last powwow at the office.

Frank Howe, a top hand and sort of straw boss, caught his night horse and staked him out at the end of a picket rope. Even when there is no herd to stand guard over, one or two night horses were always tied up or staked out, in case the nighthawk got set afoot for some reason. His horse could step in a badger hole, or throw him, and the outfit would be set afoot.

They butchered a beef that evening and we sat around a big campfire roasting ribs on branding irons. I sat squatted, gnawing the juicy charred meat from a rib bone and drinking black coffee, listening to the cowpunchers swapping yarns.

Their talk was mostly about horses and cattle and men: broncs and bronc riders; cowpunchers who had gotten into trouble and quit the country to travel the Outlaw Trail.

They spoke of places like the Hole in the Wall country which lay behind the Red Wall of Powder River in Wyoming; Brown's Hole, where a man could sit his horse at the rock monument that marked the cornerstone of three states, Wyoming, Colorado and Utah; Robbers' Roost in Utah, where Butch Cassidy, the leader of the Wild Bunch, punched cows as a young man under his real name, LeRoy Parker, before he made the mistake that forced him to ride the dim trails under the rim of the Orange Cliffs; and Blue John's cabin near the Outlaw Caves on the rim, where a man could get his bearings from the Three Flat Top Buttes.

Those were names to conjure with, and tired as I was, I sat there bug-eyed and listened to tales of outlaws and shooting scrapes, train holdups, bank robberies, that went back to the days of the Daltons and Youngers and Jesse and Frank James. Some of the stories were comical, but mostly they were tragic and tinged with sadness.

I would have liked to tell them that I knew Kid Curry and had seen Butch Cassidy and the Wild Bunch a few hours after they held up the Great Northern train. But I kept my mouth shut.

I stayed till the fire died out and the last cowpuncher had left. Then I unrolled my bed and crawled in and went to sleep with the stars in my eyes.

The next morning the Circle C outfit was moving camp on a thirty miles haul to the Missouri River, to work cattle in the brushy bottomlands and in the rough badlands back from the river.

CHAPTER NINE

Little Joe of Texas

Two horsebackers rode up to camp while we were eating breakfast. One was a kid about my age, but longer legged. Both had double-rigged saddles, the kind used by cowpunchers in the Southwest. Montana cow hands rode saddles with only one cinch rigged in the middle, known as center-fire saddles.

Their horses wore the Long X brand which belonged to a big Texas spread, the Reynolds Brothers, that had just come into the Montana country. They were one of the five who would work the beef roundup.

Brewster introduced them to us as Joe Reynolds and his nephew, Little Joe. Little Joe and I shook hands awkwardly. We loaded our plates with food and took them outside the mess tent to squat on the ground. We kept sizing each other up while we ate. I finally broke the silence.

"You eat pie this early in the mornin'?" I asked.

"I eat pie anytime, day or night," Little Joe answered.

"It's raisin pie."

"I like any kind," he said with a grin, "except mud pies. I'm always hungry. Uncle Joe thinks I have a tapeworm. Threatens to worm me."

You could tell Little Joe was a Texan by the way he talked and by his high-crowned hat that was creased down the middle, instead of dented on four sides like a Montana cow hand's; and by the longer straight-shanked spurs he wore, while mine had curved shanks.

I brought out a whole pie and cut it down the middle, then into four parts to make it easier to eat. The pie sort of opened us up and we got to talking about horses and cattle, how many brands we knew. We used sticks to draw the brands in the dirt.

I had always heard them say that a brand book was a ranch kid's primer. A ranch kid might not be able to recite the alphabet from A to Z, but he could take a piece of chalk and mark on the school blackboard the brand of every big outfit in his section of the cow country.

I knew most of the big brands in Montana and some across the Canadian line. Little Joe matched it with Texas brands and some across the Mexican border.

We got to altering brands the way cattle rustlers work one brand into another iron, while we talked about different ways used by cattle thieves; like picking a hair brand with tweezers, or using a wet gunnysack and a hot iron. We made a game out of it, altering the brands in the dirt. You would have thought we had both been born and raised in Robbers' Roost.

Little Joe showed me how the biggest brand altering the cow country ever knew was worked. The changing of the famous X I T into the Star Cross.

We got so tangled up in our long rustlers ropes we didn't know we had an audience. A dozen or more cowpunchers were in behind the mess wagon watching.

"Directly you pair of hardcase cattle rustlers get done

stealing cattle," Joe Reynolds told us, "you can get off your tails and find some work to do."

We scrambled quickly to our feet, feeling silly. One of the cowpunchers had tied a hangman's knot in his rope and hung it across a cottonwood limb. The ribbing wore itself out after awhile.

"Catch your water dogs," Brewster told the outfit. "We got a big bunch of cattle to swim across the Missouri River."

By "water dogs" he meant horses that could swim.

Brewster told them he wanted only river hands who knew what to do and when to do it without being told. He didn't want any cowpuncher who couldn't handle his horse in swimming water. One good river man, he said, was worth half a dozen green hands.

There was a knack to swimming cattle and it came only from long experience. A man could drown himself and his horse, or if he hollered at the wrong time he could balk the cattle at the water's edge. A green hand could do a lot of damage in a lot of different ways.

It took a cool head and sometimes guts, even if you were an old hand at the game. If your horse quit out in midstream while swimming a bunch of cattle, you might have to grab his tail or the tail of a cow and hang on, or swim clear. If you couldn't swim, your chance of survival was cut to a narrow margin.

The current was always fast in the channel, with whirlpools and jagged rocks to rip a horse's guts, and there was a mile of white water rapids.

"I need about eight experienced river men," Brewster

told them. "The rest of you stay on this side of the river and be ready to pick up cattle we shove across."

Snowflake was leaning on the rope corral with his ears laid back. I slid my loop over his head and led him out from the bigger horses that were dealing him misery.

Brewster cocked an eyebrow at me, and said, "I don't recollect ever takin' you along when we swam the cattle."

"I won't be underfoot," I said. "I can swim." I was speaking the truth.

"Snowflake's never been across any water wider than Beaver Creek," Brewster argued.

Frank Howe spoke up. "It'll be good experience for him, Horace. I'll look after him. I'll rope that Banjo horse for him."

"Anything happens to him," Brewster was a little worried, "I might as well quit the country."

"Don't worry. I'll be right there if he gets in a tight." Howe was on my side. "Banjo is as stout as your Flaxy horse. He'll take him across without wetting his stirrups," he added.

Brewster gave in. "Guess it's okay. They want me to make a hand out of him."

When Little Joe propositioned his uncle about going along with me, he got turned down cold, and bawled out in the bargain. "One kid underfoot is enough for Brewster to worry about," his uncle said gruffly. His remark made me hot under the collar but I didn't say anything. I was sorry for Little Joe. I wanted him to come along.

CHAPTER TEN

Swimming the Cattle

Range cattle in the northwest country have a tendency to drift south when the first cold wind comes down from Canada. The drifting cattle hunt shelter in the broken badlands along the south side of the Missouri, crossing the river with their rumps to the north wind.

Outfits on the south side pick up the stray cattle and feed those that need hay. When the Chinook winds melt the snow and the green grass comes, the wintered strays are turned loose to rustle, and reps from the different outfits on the north side of the river are sent across to work on the spring roundup.

In August the river is at the low level mark. The spring calves are big and stout enough to swim, so they are rounded up with the cows and held in a fenced pasture until there is a sizeable bunch to swim across.

Lew Roberts, a Circle C cowpuncher, and one of the Circle Diamond cow hands had been on the south side of the river gathering the cows and calves that were now pastured, waiting to be brought across.

Frank Howe was riding a gelding called Brown Jug. Fred Roberts, Lew's brother, rode a big sunburnt sorrel. Jim Swain and Joe Contway and a half-breed named Jim Brown all had good river horses. The Bearpaw Pool man rode his top horse and Buck Ballinger, a rep from the Mill Iron, saddled a roan Colorado gelding. Brewster saddled Flaxy.

Howe put my saddle on Banjo's broad back without using a saddle blanket, then he grabbed my collar and the seat of my britches and before I knew it I was straddle of the horse. I must have looked like a monkey on top of Jumbo the elephant.

I heard Brewster say that the gray sky was made to order for swimming cattle. I knew that cattle didn't swim well with the sun on the water. Reflection blinds them and when they can't see ahead they get panicky.

Every man in the outfit rode the few miles to Rocky Point Crossing. Joe Reynolds was in charge of the cow hands who were staying on the north side of the river. The rest of us rode our horses onto the ferryboat.

Banjo balked about going up the gangplank. Howe had to grab the hackamore I was using instead of a bridle, and lead Banjo snubbed to his saddle horn like he was a green bronc. I felt like a horsefly on the big barrel-rumped dun horse.

By the time the slow moving ferry got across, Banjo had quit spooking, but he still had his tail grabbed and tucked in when Howe led him down the ramp. I knew if Banjo ever took a notion to buck he would throw me so high I would grow whiskers by the time I came back to earth.

When we reached the south side, Lew Roberts met us and said they had penned about two hundred cows with big calves the night before. They were dry for water and once the gate of the corral swung open they'd head for the river and nothing could stop them. It would be up to us to keep the cattle from crowding one another when the leaders stopped to drink at the river's edge, to prevent their piling up and tromping the calves underfoot.

Lew said there were a couple of hundred steers penned up in another corral, also dry for water.

Brewster decided to take the cows and calves first. He dismounted and loosened his cinch and we did likewise. Howe let out his cinch without getting off. This was a precaution against a tight cinch interfering with a horse's breathing in swimming water.

When we had all lined up on either side of the gate, Lew leaned from his horse and swung it open. Cows and calves spewed out, bawling for water.

Lew and Brewster rode ahead, fanning the leaders out in a spreading line along the riverbank. When they reached the water they rode in belly deep and reined off, one on each side of the herd.

The rest of us closed in, pocketing the cattle as they walk-bawled to water. Howe and I followed the drags and by the time we reached the river, the leaders were laned out into swimming water. Brewster rode downstream with the cattle. He called back to us, "Keep 'em coming, boys! Crowd the swing close! Don't leave any gaps!"

All the cow hands had doubled ropes or quirts swinging. Howe slapped his saddle slicker across the tails of the drinking cattle.

"Keep 'em coming!" Brewster hollered again. "Don't leave no daylight."

I knew that if the line of swimming cattle was broken and a fifteen- or twenty-foot gap of water showed, the cattle

111

would be apt to turn downstream with the swift current and there would be a pile up. A gap was dangerous.

Most of the boys had taken off their boots and tied them to their saddles. A couple had taken off their pants, just in case they had to swim for it.

I was worried about my new alligator boots getting wet so I wrapped them in my slicker and double-knotted the saddle strings.

Brewster was far ahead of the lead cows that were following his horse. Lew Roberts was riding point down current and handling his horse like he was on dry land, without touching a bridle rein. When he wanted to turn his horse, he reached an arm into the river and splashed water against the side of the animal's head, taking care not to splash it in the ears.

Big Fred Roberts rode the swing a little way behind his brother. Both were experienced river men and rode good water horses. Big Fred was singing a comical song about a white mule with a "set-fast" on his back.

We were in the broad middle of the Missouri now. Howe and I kept about twenty feet behind to keep our horses from riding the cattle. All I could see ahead was a hundred foot wide lane of heads and horns.

It was one thing to swim the river by hand and think nothing of it, but on horseback behind a herd of swimming cattle was something else, a little scary around the edges. I was tight bellied when I heard a man holler, "Help! Help! My horse quit!" It was a wild cry from up ahead on the swing.

The panicky cry for help came from the six foot, two

hundred and fifty pound Buck Ballinger, and it was the big roan Mill Iron Colorado mountain horse that was in trouble.

I caught sight of the horse as it was reined over backwards, the spade bit yanking its mouth, the front hoofs pawing water. I saw Buck go over and under water the next second, then man and horse sank like rocks below the muddy surface.

"Easy, kid!" Howe figured I was scared. "Ride a slack rein. You're ridin' a steamboat."

Big Fred Roberts had quit singing. He turned his horse back, the swift current pulling his downstream. He had a loop built in his rope that he held high above the water, his eyes searching.

It was an endless wait until Buck's head bobbed up like a waterlogged hunk of dark wood. His big arms flailed the water and he grabbed the tail of a yearling that had been jarred loose from the herd. It looked like he was trying to mount the calf and his heavy weight was pulling the animal under.

Frew sung his small loop once in an overhand throw. The noose fell across one arm and under a big shoulder as it dropped over Buck's head. Fred jerked the slack swiftly, just as the yearling went under. He headed his horse downstream, with Buck's threshing weight at the end of his taut rope dallied a turn around the saddle horn.

Jim Swain had headed downstream. When the roan gelding surfaced, Swain made a lucky grab at the trailing bridle reins. For a while it looked as if the big roan would paw Swain under with striking shod hoofs but Swain twisted its neck and head until the Mill Iron gelding went belly up, floating sideways, its head pulled back in Swain's lap. Swain's arm snaked out to pull the latigo strap, loosening the tight cinch. A moment later the roan was swimming alongside his horse. Swain was headed for a sand bar where Fred Roberts had pulled the half-drowned Buck Ballinger.

"I smashed a couple of knuckles down rockin' Ballinger to sleep," Fred told Swain. "The big ox tried to climb on behind and this horse of mine ain't broke to ride double."

"Plug that gap! Keep 'em comin'!" Brewster hollered from the north bank.

Lew Roberts and Joe Contway were kept busy plugging a twelve foot gap of open water with cattle. Then the whole herd was out of the river on the north side, milling around and bawling as the cows hunted their calves.

Brewster looked me over with a worried expression as I rode Banjo out of the river.

"You saw what happened to that big Mill Iron rep," he said. "It split the herd wide open and Contway and Roberts got the gap filled by the skin of their teeth. We could all have been in trouble. You got off lucky."

There was no sparkle in his faded blue eyes. When he told me to ride to camp and turn loose, it left no room for argument. I knew he was fit to be tied when he and Howe and the others rode off to ferry their horses and swim the steers across.

I was putting on my boots and tightening my cinch without getting off Banjo when Little Joe came over. He wanted to know what had happened.

114

I told him I didn't want to talk about it, not now anyhow. I was shivering inside my wet clothes and I broke out in a rash of duck bumps. I felt as if I were going to vomit. I had watched a man drowning. I had seen Fred Roberts rope him, and when Buck had tried to crawl up on Fred's horse, I'd seen Fred cock back a fist and hit Buck in the face. The whole picture came back with a rush, making me sick enough to lean over sideways and let the sour vomit spew out as I hung onto the saddle horn.

When I straightened up and wiped the back of my hand across my mouth I realized that Little Joe, watching me shiver and be sick, figured I was scared. He hadn't heard Brewster tell me to go to camp, and it must have looked to him like I was sneaking off because I was afraid to help swim the rest of the cattle.

That was what I was thinking when I did the only thing I could do to prove I wasn't yellow.

"I swallowed a lot of river water," I told Little Joe. "Only way to get rid of it was to puke it up." I headed Banjo for the riverbank. "See you later, Little Joe." I tried to make it sound careless but the words were screechy.

It slipped my mind I wasn't riding Snowflake when I pulled my quirt down along Banjo's flanks. The big dun snorted, grabbed his tail and jumped over the seven foot cutbank. We hung in the air for a second and having no place to go but down, Banjo landed in ten feet of water. I had both feet in the stirrups and a death grip on the saddle horn, and I must have sucked air into my lungs by instinct as we went under.

There was no time to think about anything. I kept my

eyes open and could make out the horse's head and black mane waving under water. I was getting dizzy from holding my breath and my eardrums ached with a hard, pounding pressure. Just in time Banjo surfaced and I let the wind out of my aching lungs. I was still tight in the saddle when Banjo started swimming high in the water, headed for a sand bar a hundred feet downstream where three saddled horses stood tracked.

The big dun found footing and lunged onto dry sand. Fred Roberts and Jim Swain were squatted on the ground beside Buck Ballinger who was stretched out on the sand.

I must have looked like a drowned gopher as I sat my saddle with my boots full of water. I wanted to get down but it looked like a long drop so I just sat there until Fred Roberts hauled me off and sat me down on the sand and told me to "stay put."

Buck Ballinger's skin was the color of a dead fish's belly. The stubble of black whiskers stood out like wires and his eyes were closed. He looked flabby and awful dead.

Jim Swain and Big Fred looked sort of sick and helpless. I heard myself saying, "Lift him up from under the belly, in under his lower ribs. Pump the water out of him." For some reason they did like I said.

When I first learned to swim I took a few lessons in first aid to a drowning person. I once helped pump river water out of another kid after he half-drowned when a group of us boys were swimming in the Missouri.

Now I passed on what I knew for what it was worth, while the two cowpunchers did the work. It looked like gallons of water came out before Buck began to show signs of life. After awhile he was sitting up with his back to a tree. There was a glassy look to his eyes and he couldn't get the slack pulled up in his heavy jaw as yet. There was a big green bruise where Fred had hit him in the jaw.

A couple of Circle C cow hands and Little Joe Reynolds rode out on the sand bar. They came around by dry land.

I dumped the water out of my boots, and wanted to get back on Banjo and to camp and turn loose before Brewster showed up and commenced asking questions. But the big dun looked as high as an elephant and I knew he would never stand still if I started to climb up by the saddle strings. So I turned my back and acted like I was helping Fred and Jim Swain. I wasn't ready to face Little Joe and answer the questions he was bound to ask.

Before I knew it, Brewster rode onto the sandbar. The steers had all been crossed and I knew he came to check up on the Mill Iron rep. It was too late now for me to do anything but face the music.

If Brewster saw me he gave no sign. He was looking at Buck Ballinger's big frame shiver and shake. "He didn't drown," Brewster half smiled, "after all."

"He was dead enough to bury," Fred Roberts said, "until the kid here showed up and told us how to pump the water outa him."

Brewster seemed to see me for the first time and it looked like I was in for it. But before he could open his mouth, Little Joe had to put in his two bits worth.

"You should have seen him jump that big dun off a seven foot cutbank into deep water," Little Joe said excitedly.

The way he said it you'd think I had it in mind all along.

117

It was time I took my own part, so I said, "I forgot when I swung my quirt that I was ridin' Banjo instead of Snowflake. When he jumped I grabbed the horn and hung on. I sat tight till he came up on the sandbar. It was all an accident."

Brewster seemed satisfied with my explanation. All he said was, "Give the boy a leg up, Fred, and let him get to camp."

I motioned for Little Joe to come along with me. There are times when a feller needs a friend.

It was almost noon and the cowpunchers were coming in to change horses and eat dinner. When Fred Roberts and Jim Swain showed up with Buck Ballinger wrapped in his saddle blanket riding between them, Humpy Jack helped Buck off and removed his boots and wet clothes. Buck crawled into his own bed and pulled the tarp over his head. His face was pinched and his lips blue, and his teeth were chattering.

He was getting no sympathy. He knew he pulled a boner that could have been costly. He couldn't swim a lick and had no business going along. He would no longer be welcome here. Somehow it seemed unjust and I felt sorry for him.

After noon dinner I roped and saddled Snowflake. They were going to brand the calves that had come across the river. Howe handed me some branding irons to carry.

I got the fire started and shoved the branding irons in, taking care to leave the handles out far enough so they wouldn't get too hot to handle.

Joe Reynolds and Little Joe were doing the roping. Little

Joe was riding a close-coupled chestnut Steeldust quarter horse. When he shook a loop in his ketch-rope the little cow pony commenced walking on eggs. His rope had a tie-knot that fitted over the saddle horn, and when he threw an overhand loop and head-roped a maverick, his horse turned as he jerked the loop. When the slack rope went taut he dragged the bawling maverick out a few steps and his uncle picked up both heels. The calf was stretched out on the ground ready for branding in no time flat.

Then they reversed the roping. His uncle roped the head and Little Joe picked up both hind feet with the first loop. It was like clockwork, smooth as oiled silk. They made team tying look easy.

I was sick with envy watching Little Joe rope. It would take months and years before I could ever learn to handle a rope like that Long X Texas kid did. I told him so on our way back to camp.

Buck Ballinger was gone when we got there. George L. said the big Mill Iron rep had saddled his private and drifted.

When supper was over Humpy Jack got me off to one side and showed me a law badge he took from his pocket. "You can quit feeling sorry for Buck Ballinger. I found this pinned to his undershirt. He was a detective on the trail of Kid Curry, smellin' around to see what he could find out. I had a talk with the waterlogged bounty hunter and he decided to take a long trip where the climate was more healthy." The nighthawk flipped the badge in the air and caught it, then put it back in his pocket. He told me to say nothing about it.

119

Humpy Jack took the remuda out in the gathering dusk. Little Joe said he and his uncle were pulling out for their own roundup wagon.

"See you in about a week," Little Joe said, "when the five big outfits work together at Sun Prairie. So long till then."

I told him so long and watched him and his uncle ride off. I wanted to tell him about the law badge but I knew I'd have to keep that news to myself.

I knew more than my kid's share of things that had to do with outlaws. I had been warned indirectly that there were a lot of men who claimed to be an outlaw's friend who would shoot him in the back or from ambush to get the reward money. A thousand, two thousand dollars was a lot of money to a forty-a-month cow hand who never had more than a hundred bucks in his pocket at one time.

And while Kid Curry had his share of loyal friends, the outlaw had more than a few enemies. It behooved his friends to keep what information they had buttoned up.

I had no way of knowing how many men in the outfit besides the nighthawk knew that the tough Mill Iron rep was a range detective. But I was aware of certain things. I knew that Old Tex Alford's log cabin saloon at Rocky Point Crossing was an outlaw stopping place, what was called a "blind post office," where an outlaw could leave a message or pick one up.

News along the outlaw trail was called "the rustling of the leaves." A written message could be dangerous so the news was mostly by word of mouth. Old Tex was entrusted with such messages that he passed on to the outlaw.

I had heard that the Mill Iron rep had laid over at Old Tex's place with his string of horses until the Circle C roundup moved camp to Rock Creek. He had flashed a bank roll that would choke an ox, bought drinks for whoever stopped there. Big Buck Ballinger had lied about how he had broken out of the Oklahoma Penitentiary and was on the dodge with a bounty on his hide.

I knew that Old Tex was a hard man to fool. Big Fred Roberts might have known something about Buck Ballinger's true identity when he treated him rough in the water, but if he did he never let on. Nor did Jim Swain, who had killed a man or two somewhere in the Southwest but never talked about it. If Horace Brewster knew Buck had a law badge pinned to his undershirt, he never mentioned it.

I figured a lot of them knew because no one felt sorry for the Mill Iron cow hand. "He liked to drown a good horse," they said and let it go at that.

It was what they left unsaid that tallied, and you didn't have to be too bright to add it up. Anyway you wanted to figure it, Big Buck Ballinger, cowboy detective, got off easy.

The Mill Iron would send out another rep to work with the Circle C wagon.

We were moving camp next morning. According to schedule the Circle C wagon was due to meet the other four roundup outfits at Sun Prairie in a day or two. I had Brewster's promise that I was going to see a sight that I had never before looked at, something that probably would never again occur—five roundup outfits working together on the last general roundup that would ever be held in that section of Montana. The five outfits would be working together for a week. They had elected Horace Brewster as ramrod in charge of the five roundups; an honor he rightly deserved.

I would be seeing Little Joe in a couple of days. He said I had to eat, anyhow, one meal of what he called "grits and hominy" at the Long X wagon. They had a Texas Negro cook that made cornbread that would melt in a man's mouth. His shortnin' bread was something to write home about.

I went to sleep that night wondering what was shortnin' bread, anyhow. . . ."

Gathering the Wild Brush Cattle

Working the brushy river bottoms and the badlands was a job in itself. It tried the temper and patience of man and horse.

The willow thickets along the riverbank were higher than a man's reach on horseback, and dense as a stockade, and the tangle of underbrush and vines made it impossible to ride through in places.

Along that mile stretch of winding river, hidden by the brush, were cutbanks where the swift current of the Missouri had eaten into the shore. There were other places where long narrow stretches of sandbars fingered out into the river and left shallow inlets between the sandbars and the bank.

River cattle and white-tailed deer came out on the sandbars to water in the early morning before sunup and in the evening after sundown. The cattle were as wild and spooky as the timid deer, tricky and hard to find, and harder yet to haze out into the open. Those were the cattle we were after.

The wagons camped before sundown on the riverbank at the mouth of Rock Creek. Brewster said he was going down the river to the Gregory Doney place to hire the 'breeds to spook the cattle out of the brush. Then he would go on to Tex Alford's place at Rocky Point, to hire Old Tex to handle the beef herd. Old Tex ran the ferry at Rocky Point as well as a saloon. There wasn't a better beef boss in the country.

As soon as Brewster rode away, Humpy Jack got an iron boot last from the bed wagon, and with a cobbler's hammer, pounded down the inseams of my boots that were doing damage to my ankles.

The mosquitoes along the river grew to man-eating size. They came in thick swarms. Half a dozen big piles of sagebrush smudges were in a circle around both wagons, the thick yellow smoke spreading out. All of us wore a roll of mosquito netting around the crown of our hats. We had these pulled down now to cover our faces and necks.

The gate to the rope corral was down, but even the broncs stayed inside with the sage smudge smoke thick around them.

I sat on my bedroll while my feet soaked in a basin of warm water. I swabbed the ugly looking sores with strong carbolic solution. Humpy Jack and Howe mixed some bacon grease with gall salve and axle grease, and I rubbed the salve into the raw places of my ankles. George L. tied strips from a clean flour sack around my feet for bandages.

By that time the cowpunchers were gathered around the smudge. They commenced swapping yarns, for my benefit, about men who had lost a foot or an arm from blood poisoning; a few had died. They suggested I ride the bed wagon for a few days, to save my feet from having to be cut off.

I finally told them that if I was going to die, I would die in the saddle with my boots on. I had picked up a lot of

124

plain and fancy cuss words and I used them all. I was bawling and fighting mad and that was what they wanted.

They began giving Humpy Jack advice: Fill the boots with white beans and pour water in and the beans would swell up and stretch the damp leather. But he would have to keep a close watch on the swelling beans or they'd bust the seams wide open. They suggested that dried prunes or apples soaked in water might do the trick.

I quit cussing and managed a grin. It wasn't much of a grin but it did the trick. They quit ribbing me.

It was dark when the horses commenced drifting out of the rope corral to graze in the sagebrush smoke. Snowflake had come out a long time ago to stand behind my bedroll. He didn't like being chouched around by the other horses. He stood where the smudge was thickest, switching his tail and rubbing his head along my back to scrape off the blood-filled mosquitoes.

When Humpy Jack took the remuda out for the night, it was time to go to bed. We spread our beds near the smudge and rigged the netting on sticks over our pillows.

Brewster was in the mess tent before daybreak drinking coffee when George L. hollered "grub pile!" He had brought back a gunny sack full of catfish that Gregory Doney's womenfolk had gutted and skinned. George L. fried the fish in a big iron skillet.

Fried catfish and sourdough biscuits soaked in choke-cherry syrup made a roundup breakfast you couldn't have bought in the finest restaurant in the world.

Brewster said we'd better get moving, that we had a long hard day ahead, which was an understatement if ever there was one. We scattered out along the river at the edge of the brush a little after daybreak and were told to sit our horses and wait.

From the edge of the brush a mile wide stretch of cleared bottomland reached to the long, bare hogback ridges that sloped down through the badlands. Giant cottonwoods, a hundred years old, were scattered hit-and-miss along the lush bottom that was under water in the spring when the river overflowed its bank. Some of the bottomland had been cleared and hay was cut and stacked on the high land above the high-water marks.

The log cabin, barn and big winter cattle shed at the Rock Creek ranch hugged the ridges almost a mile away and that was where we were to drive the wild cattle as they were spooked out of the brush by the half-breeds. The five-strand barbwire fence fanned out toward the river and formed a barrier to hold the cattle.

It was still and quiet as we waited. Brewster had ridden down the river to where Gregory Doney was waiting a mile below with his tribe.

Frank Howe said, "Horace is stealin' some of Teddy Roosevelt's thunder. Teddy used natives in Africa to beat drums to spook big game out of the jungles."

The noise started directly. The shrill sounds of the women and kids were almost drowned out by the noise of sticks drumming on big tin coal oil cans and dishpans. The din sent echoes into the badlands as the volume of noise increased.

Cow hands were having their hands full trying to con-

126

trol their spooked horses. Some started pitching and even Snowflake wanted to stampede.

A bunch of white-tailed deer raced in high leaping jumps for the safety of the badlands. A bobcat sprang into the lower limbs of a cottonwood tree and crouched there, pale yellow eyes glinting.

Then the brush started cracking and the terrified brush cattle ran out from every opening they could find in the dense thicket; wild-eyed cows with calves following, steers hooking their way out. A renegade bull crashed through, vines trailing from his horns. They poured out from all sides, until the whole clearing seemed filled with wild cattle.

The tin can hammering and the screaming of the 'breeds followed close behind the spooked-out cattle, a moving wall of hideous sound.

The cowpunchers, with the help of Gregory Doney and a dozen of the older 'breed boys, spurred their horses to bunch the running cattle and turn the leaders, and the fast moving herd was funneled into the wings of the cattle trap.

The bottomland was pitted by stump holes and a big steer up-ended and crashed heavily, its neck broken. A half-breed's horse stepped into a hole and somersaulted, throwing the rider high into the air.

Snowflake shied to one side and cleared the edge of a hole with a long jump that came near throwing me. I made a lucky grab at the saddle horn as my boot slid from the right stirrup. I yanked myself back and my foot found the lost stirrup just in time.

By the time we crowded the drags through the gate the

cattle were milling, hooking sideways, strings of slobber-like wet cobwebs trailing from their bawling mouths.

There must have been fifty half-breed women and girls in gay colored dresses and moccasins, all talking and laughing at once, and that many youngsters in faded shirts and Levi's and bare feet. They had dropped the tin cans in the brush, and they were all squealing with laughter.

There was a satisfied grin on Brewster's sweaty face. He told Gregory to butcher the steer with the broken neck. Gregory sent one of his boys for a wagon to load the beef, then herded his womenfolk and kids back on foot.

We rode to camp and unsaddled and ate an early noon dinner.

There were calves and some mavericks to brand that afternoon, and when Brewster dumped his dinner plate into the dishpan, that was the signal to go.

We finished the branding and followed Brewster and Howe on a long circle into the broken badlands country.

The badlands were hard to work—scrub pines and brush, short box canyons, cut coulees and short hogback ridges, gip water springs with white alkali-crusted black bogs. There were places where a rider and horse would sink out of sight in a bottomless black bog.

I had listened to strange tales about the black bog holes in the Montana badlands, the glistening white crust that seals its dead and holds its gruesome secret in mud as black as sin. Outlaws on the dodge, who knew the badlands, were said to use it for a hideout. Indians on the warpath had led cavalry details into the badlands for an ambush trap.

Wolves and mountain lions had their dens in the hidden caves under shelving rimrocks. Clay buttes, eroded by the winds and rains of centuries, took on the shape of monuments.

Crystal clear springs had the taste of bitter quinine, others a sulphur taste and odor.

The badlands of Montana was a strange, forbidding place. Its stillness held a secret threat and warning, its nights filled with sounds—the howl of a wolf atop a bare pinnacle, the woman-scream of a mountain lion. I had seen a pair of blacktail bucks, horns locked in deadly combat, until from sheer exhaustion trying to free the antlers, they had gone down in a death grip.

A hundred foot cliff was near the head of the breaks, and at the base of the cliff the bleached bones and massive skulls of hundreds of buffalo were piled and scattered. The immense bone pile marked the old "buffalo run" where the Indians had stampeded the herds in a wholesale slaughter to get meat for the hungry tribes.

Bats roosted inside the dark caves. Birds of prey—hawks, eagles and owls—nested in the rimrocks and the stunted scrub pine and buckbrush. No songbird greeted the sunrise or warbled its evening carol at the close of day.

To me, young as I was, the broken badlands seemed a desolate country, offering a last haven for hunted animals and outcast men.

We came out of the brakes about sundown with a handful of cattle. The cowpunchers cussed the country as they rode tired horses. They were willing to give it back to the Indians.

Humpy Jack and I went for a swim before he took the remuda out for the night. We built a smudge on the bank before we shed our clothes.

The moonlight on the water turned the old Missouri River into quicksilver. The fragrance of wild roses filled the night. Muskrats swam in and out of their holes, and I could hear the slap-slap of beaver tails where they were building a dam downstream where Rock Creek emptied into the river.

We dressed in the smoke of the smudge and I rubbed salve on my ankles that were beginning to heal. We ate chokecherries until our mouths puckered.

The cattle were inside the fence and there was no night guard to stand. I unrolled my bed and rigged the mosquito netting in place and crawled in.

If any mosquitoes got through the netting they got a bellyful because I was dead to the world till George L. hollered "grub pile" at daybreak next morning.

I pawed the tarp off my face, knuckled the sleep out of my eyes and pulled on my Levi's and boots and rolled up my bed, going through the motions like a sleepwalker.

I shoved my head and face into a basin of cold water, and dried off, and was still half asleep when I filled my tin plate and cup in the mess tent, the only place in camp where there was a light. I went out into the dark and sat on the ground with my back against the front wheel of the mess wagon. The remuda inside the rope corral was no more than a black blot.

Humpy Jack Davis, the nighthawk who had been in the saddle all night, was the only man in camp fully awake, but he had sense enough not to do any talking. The average cowhand isn't fit company for man or beast till he's had his second cup of black coffee and his first smoke. Somebody once said the makers of Four X Arbuckle coffee and Bull Durham tobacco deserved a rawhide crown for the part they played in a cow camp in the early West.

When Brewster dropped his empty plate and cup and eating tools into the big battered dishpan, that meant breakfast was over at the Circle C wagon.

It was almost an hour until daylight when the cowpunchers roped their circle horses. If a man lit a match it was to see if he had caught the right horse.

Snowflake was outside the corral where he wanted to be. Humpy Jack had let him dodge back when he corraled the remuda. That little white cow pony figured he was hid out in the shadow of the bed wagon. He'd have crawled under it like a hound if he thought he could make it. As it was, he acted like a kid caught playing hooky when I bridled and saddled him.

A couple or three horses with humps in their backs pitched a few jumps, grunting and squealing. I stayed close to Brewster while he waited for the last man to get mounted. Then we rode off at a long trot in the lead of the others.

We pulled up on a little rise to wait for the cowpunchers from the other outfits. Brewster pointed out the different camps that were spaced about a half mile apart, to give the remudas plenty of room to spread out and graze without fear of mixing. Each outfit had its day herd of four-year-old beef steers spread out and grazing, with a couple of cowpunchers on each day herd.

There was the Circle Diamond, with John Survant, general manager for the big spread owned by the Bloom Cattle Company, ramrodding the wagon.

The Bear Paw Pool outfit, representing a dozen or more smaller outfits in the Bear Paw Mountains, was camped a mile beyond. Tom McDonald was running the Bear Paw wagon.

The Milner Square, with Bill Jaycox as wagon boss, was next. And at the far end was the Long X, with Joe Reynolds ramrodding his own outfit.

The Circle C camp was at the far end of the line of roundup wagons, with Horace Brewster as wagon boss.

From where we sat our horses on the rim of a high benchland, Sun Prairie stretched out about ten or twelve miles wide and as far as the eye could see to the north and south. The scrub timbered Larb Hills to the east made a formidable background. They were an extension of the badlands of the Missouri River that flattened out toward the north into the rolling plains that were lost to sight in the summer haze. The prairie land reached to the Milk River Valley and extended still further to the Cypress and Sweetgrass Hills in Alberta, across the Canadian border.

Brewster's arm made a wide, sweeping motion toward the north where Sun Prairie widened and the whole country was spread out in an endless rack to the east and west. "That's cow country," he said, musingly. "Wide, open range, where the grass touches a man's stirrups. A cow country where a man ahorseback can travel a week without seein' a barbwire fence."

He rolled a cigarette as we sat our horses and viewed the panoramic scene.

"Ten or fifteen years from now," he prophesied, "the open range you're lookin' at now will be under fence. There's already talk of the dry land farmers moving in and fencing the open range in other parts of the country. It'll happen here, too, and when it does, I hope to God I won't be alive to see it."

It was hard for me to believe that dire prophecy, but I knew it was true and something of the warmth of the summer sun was gone and the blue sky had faded like the old cowhand's eyes were dimmed.

I was fourteen years old but as the tragic sadness and bitterness of Brewster's words sank in deep, I suddenly felt grown up and old and disillusioned. I hoped I wouldn't be here to see the cow country plowed under.

There was a vastness there that crept into my young cowboy heart and into my blood. The sun and alkali dust and the smell of sage, the cured bunch and buffalo grasses, and the worn buffalo trails that streaked the long ridges.

It was cow country the day I saw it.

CHAPTER TWELVE

First Day's Roundup at Sun Prairie

We hadn't long to wait on the rim overlooking Sun Prairie before the other outfits showed up.

The ramrod of each wagon rode in the lead of his cowpunchers and they pulled up beside Brewster and me where we sat our horses. The cowboys from the various outfits milled around aimlessly, greeting men they had not seen in a long time. There was a lot of rough joshing back and forth, while Brewster gave the ramrods their orders about which way to ride on the long morning circle.

Little Joe and I found one another in the dim light, but we didn't have time to talk before the ramrods leading circle rode off, calling to their crew of cow hands to follow.

There must have been more than a hundred cow hands in that big gathering that rode away in the early dawn. Cigarettes glowed like fireflies. The jingle of spur rowels and the creak of saddle leather and the stomp of shod hoofs, all fading now in the distance.

It was a long twenty-five mile circle that morning. Brewster kept dropping the Circle C men off in pairs till there was nobody left but him and me on the outside circle.

The sun was two hours high when we picked up our little drive of cattle and headed back toward the holdup

134

ground on Sun Prairie. We had gathered about a hundred head.

"There'll be a big herd to work when all the drives come in," Brewster explained to me. "So when we eat dinner and get a change of horses we'll split the big gatherment into five parts and each outfit will work a separate herd, cutting the cows with unbranded calves first and holding them in one bunch. The four-year-old steers will be cut into another holdup, then the beef steers will be cut and held in a separate day herd."

It sounded simple and easy the way Brewster told it, but before sundown I was to see how that simple, easy equation was to work out in a bewilderment of dust and bawling cattle and men on sweat-marked horses.

When we came off a wide ridge with our drive we could see a dozen other drives stringing in from benchlands and ridges, through draws and coulees, in bunches from fifty to a hundred head. It was like the spokes of a wheel centered to a large hub, the hub the holdup ground on the level stretch of prairie.

The walk-bawl of a thousand cattle spread its sound in all far-flung directions. Cowboys hollered back and forth and slapped quirts along their chaps. Clouds of alkali dust puffed up from shuffling cloven hoofs. Weary horses, dried sweat coating their hides, traveled with slowed-down gait from the long morning circle. The faces and clothing of the riders were dirt grimed.

The five roundup camps beyond the spreading herd, on the sagebrush and greasewood flat, came into sight in the dust pall, the noonday high sun transforming the stretch of prairie into a golden haze.

We eased our drive into the big herd on the flat and rode around at a slow walk while the cow hands held the cattle loose-bunched.

Cows that had become separated from their calves were horning their way, bawling for their calves and the lost calves kept answering. Finally a cow would find her stray calf and muzzle it all over, and when she made certain it was her own she would let it suckle while her rough tongue cow-licked its hide.

The cows with unbranded calves were to be cut from the herd after we'd ridden to camp for noon dinner and a change of horses. By that time every cow would have found her own calf.

As far as I knew I had only Snowflake to ride and I felt pretty mean about riding him back to the herd. I was feeling a little sorry for myself as I went to camp with Brewster.

I was about to loosen the saddle cinch and tie Snowflake to the wheel of the bed wagon, when he told me to turn loose. I wondered why I was being set afoot but I asked no questions and did as I was told.

"I managed a string of horses for you," Brewster told me, sort of offhand while we were eating dinner. Then he named them: Corbett, Pryor, Smith, Nig, Buster, Snip, Pipe, Possum and the Sun River Black.

I knew each horse and could have described them all if he had asked me.

"Bob and Will didn't think you deserved your own

string," he told me. "Seems like somebody saw you asleep and the remuda spilled."

"That's right," I answered honestly. "If it hadn't been for Jack Davis the outfit would be camped there yet, hunting horses."

"Your father argued in your favor," Brewster said. "And what the nighthawk told Bob and Will cooled them off."

The glad news about my string of horses was soured. I knew I would get jumped out by Bob and Will for spilling the remuda. I dumped my plate in the dishpan and left before George L. could get the pie he said he'd cached for me in the mess box.

I put my bridle on Corbett and saddled him. He was harder to get on than Snowflake, but I made it somehow without grabbing the saddle strings. Perhaps it was the high-heeled boots that helped, or maybe it was because I was rankled. Anyhow, I swung up and from that time on I never used my saddle strings to climb aboard. I'd finally got the knack of it, despite my short legs and runty size.

By the time we got back to the holding grounds, the big herd had been split into five parts. Each herd was about a half mile apart in order not to interfere with the cutting and slashing and whittling that had to be done.

A heavy pall of dust hung over what seemed the entire stretch of Sun Prairie, so thick I couldn't see the tents and wagons of the different camps. By the time we got to the loose-bunched cattle we were to work I could barely make out the other four bunches.

Brewster took me into the herd with him to work out the cows and calves. We rode side by side at a walk till we spotted a cow with her calf, then we worked them slowly toward the edge and laned them out to where the cow hands holding the herd would pick them up and head them for the cut. Then we rode back in for another cow and calf. It was slow work that called for patience and cow-savvy. Sometimes we had to pull up and wait till a cow found her calf, because there could be no mistake about a cow claiming the calf that belonged to her. I was glad when we finished and rode out of the herd.

Brewster waved to the reps to go in and cut their own cows and calves, then we rode off a way and got down and loosened out tight cinches. Our horses were already sweat-marked, and we were dust-powdered, our eyes red-lidded and bloodshot and itchy from the alkali dust.

When the reps had finished I rode in with Brewster to cut the four-year-old beef steers. Cutting steers is a one-man job but Brewster took me along to show me how to get the job done.

By the time we were finished cutting the four-year-old steers the bunch of cows and calves had been driven off to a big corral. The branding irons were hot in the cow chip fire and the cattle bawling when we got there.

The horse wrangler had led Brewster's roping horse and tied him up. When he unsaddled and changed horses, the wrangler led his cutting horse away and turned him loose in the remuda. Brewster and one of the reps did the calf roping.

I kept the calf tally in Brewster's tally book and tended the branding fire while the calf branding was going on.

It was sundown when we got back to camp and turned

our horses loose. I was feeling hungry by then. I had sloughed off whatever was gnawing at me and watched my shadow as I rode to camp, admiring what I saw.

Frank Howe was leading Possum out of the corral. "You're on first guard with Howe," Brewster said as we rode in.

Frank Howe was a big, powerful six-footer, towheaded, with a smashed nose. There was a grin on his wide mouth when I put my rope over Possum's head. He said, "Possum's got cat eyes on a dark night. Best night horse in the remuda. He's out of my string."

I got it then. Brewster had taken one horse out of each man's string to give to me. I didn't like it.

"The boys made up a horse pool," Howe said quickly when he saw the look on my face. "They gave you the smallest horse in each string, and Brewster gave each his pick from the extra string."

I was glad to know I hadn't set any man afoot for a mount.

Howe started singing as we left camp. He kept it up for the most part of two hours night guard, and never sang the same song twice. Some were old cowboy ballads, with endless verses, most of them ribald. Others were sentimental love songs, some old and some new. Others were songs from minstrel shows, coon songs they were called.

So I listened to Howe's songs that night as we rode around the bedded cattle. There wasn't more than a hundred head, all told, and as a rule a small herd is harder to hold at night than a big one, but the boys on cocktail guard had watered the steers and let them graze onto the bedground with full paunches. The night was mild, the stars out, and the moon yellow.

There was a great fascination for me riding around the bedded herd on a star-filled night. I liked the smell of the cattle and the pungent odor of sage, and the faraway sky line of the open range. I also liked to hear the cattle chewing their cuds in full-bellied contentment.

The songs Howe sang conjured up dreams as I rode at an easy gait and listened to the creak of saddle leather and the faint tinkling of spur rowels. A lone coyote on a distant hill broke the silence with its yapping, and when a second coyote answered it seemed like a dozen joining the chorus. Then there was a vacant echo in the night.

A strange loneliness touched my young cowboy dreams and a plaintive sort of sadness gripped me as I remembered a pile of rocks on a hill that marked some cowboy's grave. I wondered who the man was and how he had died and been buried by men who had shared a part of his life.

A rock piled monument to mark the lonely grave. A cowboy song to recount the saga whenever his kind gathered around campfire or bunkhouse.

The West was as young that night as the boy who rode guard, but no younger in heart than the grizzled cow hand who passed along to me in his songs the legend of the cowboy and the cow country.

That two-hour night guard passed before I was aware of it. Howe took a look at the big silver-cased guard watch that belonged to Horace Brewster. "Five minutes till ten," he said, "and the shank of the evenin'. Ride to camp and wake the two men on second guard."

140

I rode to camp and tried to be quiet about it. I knew where the two men on second guard had unrolled their beds. I shook them awake and unsaddled Possum and led him off a way before turning him loose. Humpy Jack Davis had told me when I got to camp just to turn Possum loose and he'd find the remuda. When I slid the headstall off, sure enough that wise night horse headed at a trot for the horse cavy.

I tiptoed, careful not to wake George L., when I filled my cup with lukewarm coffee he had set on the stove. I found the raisin pie where he said it would be under a dishtowel. I ate about half the pie and was washing it down with a second cup of coffee when Blackstrap showed up for his ten o'clock snack.

I cut up a piece of meat for him and scratched behind his ears while he chewed. When he climbed back on the wagon seat it was time to go to bed. I was bedded down behind the mess tent and pulling the tarp over my head when Howe rode into camp. I was dead to the world by the time he unsaddled and turned his horse loose. I had left the rest of the pie where he would find it, and that ended my responsibilities for the day.

I figured I earned my dollar and thirty-three and a third cents of my forty-a-month pay since saddling my pony at four that morning.

Tomorrow was another day and four in the morning comes early.

CHAPTER THIRTEEN

Roping Sheep with Little Joe

Frank Howe led circle the next morning. Little Joe Reynolds and I were dropped off together about halfway around what Howe said would be a forty mile circle.

I was riding the Sun River Black. Little Joe was forking a chestnut sorrel, short-coupled cow pony. We rode along watching our shadows and talking, not paying too much attention to the rough country. We were on the lookout for cattle but there wasn't so much as a wind-belly poddie orphan calf in sight, so we started roping at clumps of sagebrush and greasewood as we went along, swapping yarns like a pair of seasoned old hands trying to outlie one another.

The tinkle of bells put an end to the tall tale telling. When we topped the next rise we knew it was sheep bells. We could see the band of woollies spread out grazing, the herder squatted on a hilltop with his two shepherd dogs.

We pulled up and listened to the blatting. We got to talking about how a band of sheep would graze across the cow country, cropping the bunch grass down to the roots, making it unfit for cattle range until the grass grew back again next spring or the year after. No wonder the cattlemen hated sheep.

We talked about stampeding the band of sheep over a

high bluff, like the Indians had the buffalo. But there was no high bluff in sight. So we decided to practice roping a few.

It was a quarter mile to where the sheepherder and his dogs sat on the hill. As we rode into the edge of the band of woollies, the loops shook out in our ketch-ropes, we tried to get a little bunch cut off and running. But they stood in a tight knot, heads down, scared and sulled. The sheep must have been used to horsebackers because we wasted half a dozen loops that just bounced off their backs.

We charged another bunch, hollering to spook them. One bell sheep trotted and I took after it, swinging a loop big enough to rope a longhorn steer as I closed the gap.

I never knew for sure whether the sheep went through the loop or if I missed. I heard the crack of the sheepherder's rifle and the whine of a 30-30 bullet. At the sound of the gunshot, the Sun River Black took off across country, cold-jawed and grabbing his tail. The small grazing bit couldn't begin to hold him and I didn't have enough strength to pull him up.

Little Joe was riding at a lope, swinging his rope at a black sheep. I passed him like he was standing still. I dropped my ketch-rope and made a grab at my hat as it started to slide off. It was an old black, wide-brimmed, high-crowned hat I had found in the bed wagon and decided to wear to save my own. It was a few sizes too large and I had used half a dozen lantern wicks for padding under the sweatband. I yanked it down too hard and it stuck across my eyes and stayed there, the wide brim flopping up and down.

143

When the brim flapped up against the hat crown I got a snapshot glimpse of the sheepherder. He was standing up now, a long-legged man with long dirty yellow hair and whiskers, a rifle in both hands. It looked like the Sun River Black was headed up a long draw, straight at the locoed sheepherder, and I was too scared to do anything but hang on with everything I had. The sheep had scattered and as near as I could tell I was in the broad middle of the band.

I sighted a cutbank fifty feet ahead, where the rains had washed down the cut coulee. It looked like a twenty foot drop and twenty feet across. I was too scared to kick my feet out of the stirrups and let the stampeding, cold-jawed horse throw me. I sat frozen in the saddle, numb with the stark fear that glued me there, my brain paralyzed, as I saw the deep wide gap coming at me. I must have ducked my head because the wide floppy brim came down across my face and it was like riding a pitching bronc with a black blindfold across my eyes.

When the horse jumped the washout and landed running on the other bank I wasn't aware of it. Everything was happening in split seconds but time had lost all measurement. When the hat brim flipped up, there were no longer any sheep, and no sheepherder with a rifle.

The Sun River Black had run himself down in a blind coulee filled with buckbrush. Ahead was a high clay cutbank and on either side the coulee was thick and matted. The horse was dripping sweat and blowing as he stood there, head lowered.

I was breathing hard and I could feel and hear my heart pounding and thumping, and that was the only sound I could hear. I was shaking so badly it took me a while to get the hat pulled off my head, where it was glued down like a suction cup. Once I got it off I wasn't going to put it on again but I was scared to throw it away, for fear it might start the horse off on another cold-jawed run.

I was so afraid of the horse by now that I was scared to move in the saddle. Finally I inched the hat down across my belly without moving my arms, and shoved it into the belt of my chaps. I was nerving myself to get off and walk, when the Sun River Black braced his legs and shook himself. I had to grab hold of the saddle horn with both hands to keep from being shaken off, I was so weak-kneed. Then he started back at a running walk along the dim trail out of the coulee.

I sat tight in the saddle and pulled my head in and shut my eyes as the brush raked my face. The trail rimmed out on a bald clay ridge and I knew that I was hopelessly lost on top of a horse I was afraid of.

Then little Joe rode into sight. As I watched him coming toward me, some of my courage ebbed back.

"What got into you?" he wanted to know, looking about as scared as I felt, "chargin' off thataway straight for that locoed sheepherder."

"My horse cold-jawed on me," I blurted out the truth.

"I thought you was a goner," Joe said. "That crazy sheepherder kept shootin', then he sicked his dogs on us. If ever they find out at camp that we got run off by a sheepherder, the cowpunchers will never let up on us. We'll never live it down in a hundred years."

"There's no need in anybody findin' out," I said. I was

more worried about the Sun River Black stampeding than I was about being joshed.

"If ever I ride this thing again," I told Joe, "I'll use a spade bit on him."

"I'd sooner ride a bronc than a broke horse that'll cold-jaw and stampede with a man," he said.

I agreed with him. Right there and then Little Joe Reynolds became my friend. I took a little courage from his words. A lot of men could have hinted that I was a rank coward—call me Man Afraid of his Ponies.

We headed back for the holdup grounds and I gave the black his head, hoping he would have horse sense enough to head for camp.

"You got any idea where camp is?" asked Joe.

"No more than you have," I told him. I knew that we got lost getting out of range of the sheepherder's rifle.

We topped a little rise and there was the sheepherder's tent. He was dry camped a mile from water. You could see where he had bedded his sheep on the slope of the hill directly behind the tent.

"Serve that crazy sheepherder right if I was to set fire to his stinkin' tent," Joe said.

I said it might start a prairie fire.

We rode up to the tent and dismounted. I reckon both of us had the same notion, to wreck the camp and destroy what there was, but we talked ourselves out of the idea.

We had both been brought up to hate and despise sheep and sheepherders and all sheepmen. Sheep destroyed the cattle range. All sheepherders, we were told, ate loco weed

146

and were half crazy. The sheep owners were no more than sheepherders, with money in the bank.

Hating sheep outfits was one thing. Wrecking a sheep camp was something else. But that didn't stop us from taking a look around.

It was a known fact that sheep outfits fed better than cow outfits. We found half a case of condensed milk and six sealed cans of butter, something no cow outfit furnished on a roundup.

We took a can of butter apiece and three cans of condensed milk, wrapping the loot in our slickers tied on our saddles. I soaked the old black hat in the water barrel and put the lantern wicks back in the sweatband and fastened the wide brim to the high crown with a big safety pin I found.

The camp was neat and clean. The tarp covered bed rolled up. We didn't unroll the bed, and we let some round tins of Copenhagen snuff and a box of 30-30 cartridges alone. We figured the milk and butter was payment enough for being shot at and missed. We did help ourselves to some snuff from an open can on the table, rolling it into cigarette papers, but it was too moist to burn, so we gave it up as a bad job.

"I think you chew the stuff," Joe said, "like chewing tobacco."

It seemed worth trying out, so I put some in my mouth and tongued it into my cheek. Joe took a mouthful. Just then we sighted the sheepherder and his dogs as they came over the hill, so we forked our horses as he came toward us on the run, waving his gun and hollering as he set his dogs on us.

I clean forgot about the horse cold-jawing as we hit a long lope. But the Sun River Black had worn the run out of his system. As we rode along I kept spitting out the saliva as it crawled into my mouth. My cheek burned from the wet wad of snuff and the sweet taste was making me feel sick. My head felt dizzy and ballooned out, and I began to break out in a cold sweat. I turned my head away from Little Joe and spewed out the wet wad.

I looked back across my shoulder. The sheepherder was on a little hill, still shooting at us. I could hear the crack of his gun inside my dizzy head as I hung onto the saddle horn and leaned sideways to vomit.

As I was retching I caught glimpses of Little Joe. He was leaning across the saddle horn and upchucking along the neck of his loping horse.

The horses stopped at the edge of a creek. I don't remember getting off, but there I was, flat on my belly, retching and shivering, clammy cold with sweat. And Little Joe was beside me in the same miserable fix. If the sheepherder had come on us then he would have caught the pair of us helpless, afoot, and at his mercy.

After a while we managed to crawl to the edge of the creek and shove our heads into the cool water. We rinsed the slime out of our mouths and drank. When we sat up and looked at each other, we tried to grin. But if my face looked anything like Joe's, it wasn't worth the effort to die game.

"We'd better high-tail it before that sheepherder smokes us out," I managed to say.

"Even if we knew where camp was," Little Joe said, "we wouldn't dare show up, the shape we're in."

"We can travel till we kinda get our bearings," I said, "then get off and lie down if we can. All we got to do is follow Killed Woman Creek till we sight the wagons."

We examined our horses for bullet wounds as we rode along, building up a scary story that would have rivaled any windy Frank Howe ever spilled around a campfire. We were feeling a little better when we heard the sound of bawling cattle being driven in the broken hills.

"If Uncle Joe is on that drive and finds me," Little Joe said miserably, "I'll get my tail in a sling."

"I guess we'd better not get off our horses to rest," I said.

We were going to feel plenty ashamed coming in empty-handed from our morning circle. We tried our best to make up some sort of an excuse for not fetching in any cattle, but none of them sounded like anything but lies. We knew they would think we had couleed up somewhere and gone to sleep.

Misery likes company and we shared it for all it was worth as we headed for the cattle drive that came into sight. We were as sorry a pair of scared young cowboys as you would find between the Mexican border and the Canadian line.

Little Joe commenced jerking his saddle strings. "We better get rid of this canned stuff before they find out we robbed a sheep camp," he suggested.

I told him I'd take it off his hands. Added to mine it made a big bulge in my saddle slicker. I knew if I was caught with it I would never be able to lie out of it.

We picked up the drag end of the drive and hoped nobody saw us.

CHAPTER FOURTEEN

On Day Herd with Old Tex

Brewster put me on day herd. He said old Tex would teach me how to handle a beef herd. A good beef boss's job was to put tallow on the steers and he drew top wages for it.

Old Tex and I rode out to the herd after breakfast. He always made it a point to be there before the cattle stirred off the bedground.

When the two cowpunchers on last guard headed for camp, we sat our horses in the gray dawn, waiting for the steers to get up of their own accord. As Old Tex explained it, you graze the beef herd all day and let them take their time watering. You graze them onto the bedground with a full paunch and all the water they can hold.

"That's when the beef steers put on taller," he told me. "The longer they stay on the bedground, the more taller they put on their ribs." He said a thousand head would put on two pounds apiece a night. At six cents a pound that would be a hundred and twenty dollars a night increase. Ten nights would be twelve hundred. A man could figure it out for himself.

"But it could all be chouced off in an hour if something got the cattle off the bedground, and there'd go the profits," he said. "That's why I never let a cow hand practice swinging a loop at the heels of a steer," he added.

On a beef roundup every ounce of meat counted. That was why a beef steer was carefully handled. Rough handling could knock off in a day the taller it took months to put on.

The sun was up by the time the herd was up and grazing. Old Tex kept cocking his head sideways to look up at the sky and the clouds that were gathering along the sky line.

"You better ride to camp," he told me. "Leave word with the nighthawk and George L. that we're movin' camp. They can tell Brewster I'm beddin' the herd high up yonder on the bench above Dry Beaver. It'll be a dry camp. The horse wrangler had better fill the water barrels."

Old Tex pointed toward the black-edged thunderheads pushing over the sky line. "Sometime after sundown she's goin' to come a bad storm," he warned.

I sighted Little Joe Reynolds as I rode past the Long X camp. He waved his hat and loped out to head me off. He looked plenty worried.

"You ever hear of a gun slinger named Jack Teal?" he asked. "He's wearin' a law badge and he's hired out for a tough hand to the sheepmen. I think he saw us yesterday. I figured I'd better tip you off."

"I'm gettin' rid of the canned stuff," I said, "as quick as I get to camp. All we can do is sit tight and say nothing."

I invited Little Joe to ride to camp with me and talk George L. out of a pie. As we rode in we saw a saddled horse near the mess wagon. There was a Winchester carbine in the saddle scabbard and we knew that no working cow hand on the roundup ever packed a saddle gun.

Little Joe and I swapped quick looks as we reined up. We were about to ride off when the man came out of the mess tent, with a tin plate in his hand piled with grub. He wore a cartridge belt with a holstered six-shooter slanted across his lean flanks and a law badge pinned to his shirt pocket.

He was a hatchet-faced, mean-eyed man who needed a shave. Both cheeks bulged as if he had a bad case of mumps. His spur rowels jangled as he stomped out of the tent and came around the rear wheel of the mess wagon. He threw the grub, plate and all, into the brush.

The law officer was making choking sounds and his watery eyes bugged out like a hoptoad as he bent double and spat out whatever bulged his jaws.

George L. came out, a faint grin on his face and a meat cleaver gripped in his hand. "Drop around any time, Teal," he said, waving the meat cleaver. "It ain't every roundup camp has grizzly stew for dinner. You said somethin' about wanting a look at the pelt."

"Wait," the law man worked at his teeth with a turkey quill toothpick. "Just wait till I get hold of lyin' Frank Howe." His voice sounded gritty as he picked up his bridle reins and swung into the saddle. He kept spitting and coughing as he rode off. He was too mad and upset to take any notice of us.

I heard a cackling laugh behind me. Humpy Jack had his red head poked out the fly of his tepee. "That Howe was braggin' to Teal how George L. could build the best mutton stew a man ever threw into a hungry belly. So Teal high-tailed it here to sample the sheep meat." The night-hawk's cackling laugh followed the law rider out of sight.

"I doctored that stew," George L. chuckled. "I told him I'd dig up the pelt when he finished eating." He laid the meat cleaver on the rawhide covered table and brought out a raisin and apple pie. He motioned for us to get down and tie into it.

"Teal is on the prowl for the cowboys who roped some sheep and robbed the sheep camp," he said. "There was blood in his eye when he rode up. I poured some croton oil into the stew and seasoned it with hot pepper sauce. Teal is goin' to be doubled up with cramps before long. That'll teach that gun slinger not to sit on my bedroll."

Unless the weather was bad George L. wouldn't let any-body but the wagon boss eat inside the mess tent. Like all roundup cooks, he was set in his ways and cranky at times. The mess tent was a roundup cook's castle, and Heaven help the man who sat on his rolled bed.

I suddenly remembered why I'd been sent to camp. I gave Humpy Jack and George L. the message Old Tex had sent for Brewster to move camp that evening.

"Old Tex says it's coming up a bad storm," I told them.

George L. took a look at the blue sky overhead and called the beef boss a liar.

Humpy Jack said if the outfit was moving camp he'd better take a few hours shut-eye. He pulled his head inside the tent flap.

Little Joe and I ate our pie and rode away. We felt fairly safe. It looked like Teal didn't know the identity of the cowboys the sheepherder had shot at, and he'd have a hard time finding out.

When I got back to the day herd Old Tex was squatted on a little hill in the shade of his horse. I could tell by the way he looked up from under his hat brim that he was sulking and in a bad humor.

He had a lard pail on the ground and was spearing a hunk of meat into his mouth with the long blade of his jacknife. He motioned with his arm toward the grazing cattle.

"I reckon you had sense enough to eat while you were at camp," he said. "You were gone long enough to take a two hour nap. I seen you and that Long X kid takin' your time. This is a roundup outfit, not a schoolyard ree-cess layoff. It's time you two buttons quit horsin' around and made hands. Now ride out there and keep that little bunch from grazin' off into the coulee."

Old Tex commenced spitting and coughing. As I rode away I could hear him cussing George L. I wanted to tell the touchy old-timer what was in the mulligan that the cook had sent out with the horse wrangler, but the cranky temper he was in, I was afraid to open my mouth.

After all, I salved my conscience, Old Tex would get even with George L. in his own way. They'd been feuding for years. I'd better not butt in.

Old Tex was tough as a boot. It would take more than a bait of doctored mulligan to get him down.

I eased the beef steers back into the herd and stayed my distance.

Later when the old beef boss rode up, he was in better humor.

We watched others working the holdup as we sat our horses on the high benchland, while the cattle grazed in grass that was hock high. From where we were the whole thing was something to store away in my memory, to recall in later years. The roundup wagons, the remudas, the spread out cattle.

It was late afternoon when Brewster and a dozen cow hands shoved a bunch of four-year-old steers into the day herd we were holding. By that time the Circle C outfit had moved camp up on the bench.

The late August day had been sultry. Heat lightning now sheeted the black clouds that lay heavy on the horizon. The distant rumble of thunder was no louder than a whispering growl as yet.

"Been like that for a week," Brewster said as he rode up.

"It takes a week to clabber," Old Tex spoke with conviction. "She'll hit sometime tonight. When she does, it'll take every cow hand you got to keep this herd together. Even then we'll spill some." He squinted his eyes. "Any other outfit movin' camp," he asked.

"Not that I know of, Tex," Brewster said. "I never told the other wagon bosses I was movin' camp. I didn't know myself until I got in and Jack Davis and George L. had the wagons loaded and ready to pull out. They gave me your message and I took your word for it that it's goin' to storm."

"If that storm don't hit tonight," Old Tex drawled, "I'll quit, and the Circle C won't owe me a dollar."

Frank Howe and I were to stand night guard from two in the morning until the day herd men relieved us.

Howe had taken stock in Old Tex's mysterious powers as a weather prophet and put up the bed tent. We spread our beds inside and tried to get some sleep.

Old Tex had dumped his bed inside the tent but he said he didn't figure on using it. He expected to be in the saddle most of the night. He changed horses, ate supper and went out on cocktail guard to bed the herd down.

Both sides of the bed tent were rolled up to let in what little breeze stirred in the sultry night. Howe and I had the tent to ourselves. Brewster's bed was in the mess tent.

CHAPTER FIFTEEN

The Storm

When the first guard man came in to wake us, he said it was dark as a pocket and it had taken him a while to find camp. He gave Howe the guard watch and told him that the cattle wouldn't bed down and that Old Tex was on the prod.

Old Tex had given him orders to wake Brewster, but Horace was already up and dressed, drinking coffee in the mess tent. He ordered every man in the saddle to help hold the herd.

The moon was down and there wasn't a star to be seen in the black sky. Sheet lightning painted streaks of orange light and the broken sky line showed like sawed black cardboard. A few big raindrops hit my face as I looked up while I was tightening the saddle cinch on Possum.

Big drops of rain began to splash as Howe and I rode away from camp. I gave Possum his head and he traveled alongside Howe's horse in the pitch black.

The grass was wet before we reached the herd, the lightning a constant sheet against the black sky. The dull rumble of thunder had a heavy rolling sound. The wind was coming up.

I twisted my head to look back. Where our horses had traveled, the wet grass was a phosphorescent glow that seemed to move in our wake. The phosphorescent tail looked spooky. "Fox fire," Howe said just before the black wind at our backs caught up with us.

A heavy roll of thunder crashed around us and chain lightning split the sky with a ragged slash. There was a blinding flare, then darkness. Tiny balls of fox fire showed from the wet horn tips of the big native steers as they tossed their heads sideways as they moved. When the horns clashed as they hooked one another, the tips were like the sparks from a white-hot horseshoe on an anvil.

Across the herd those showering fireballs were an awesome sight.

A cowboy was singing a dirgelike tune a little off-key when the chain lightning split the sky and the crash of thunder shook the earth. A blinding white glare hung over the herd that were riding one another in their animal terror, broad wet backs and horns shining and polished. Steers bawled crazily, slobber stringing like trailing cobwebs from their mouths, the whites of their eyes rolling.

The whole herd had come untracked in one split second's timing. They were on the move, walk-bawling in a jam-packed mass.

I caught sight of Old Tex riding the point on the far side. Three cow hands in shining wet yellow slickers were bunched behind the old beef boss, coiled ropes in their hands, whipping the lead steers over their heads to turn the leaders back, in an effort to get the cattle milling before they started running.

Then the bright glare was gone, as if drowned out in the heavy windswept cloudburst. It was as if the chain lightning had ripped open the low-hung black sky. The gale drove the sheets of rain like the swift current of a black river.

The rolling crash of thunder was loud and continuous. Lightning ripped the sky in half a dozen places. The whole benchland was one vast lake that looked like a sea of moving quicksilver. The herd was moving hock deep in mud and dirty water. Bolts of chain lightning stabbed at the metallic sea, huge curtains of sheet lightning smeared the whole sky, thunder claps met and sent back deafening echoes.

Howe's shout alongside me had a far-off sound as he crowded his horse close. I couldn't make out the words but I knew he was crowding me away from the milling cattle.

I caught sight of Brewster when a sheet of lightning lit up the whole scene. He and the other cowpunchers were strung out, slapping at the cattle with slickers.

I was too scared to do anything but sit tight in the saddle and ride. I didn't know I was holding a tight rein on Possum until Howe leaned over and jerked the bridle reins from my grip and dropped them over my saddle horn.

If I'd been numb with fear before, it was nothing compared to the hopeless terror I felt now. Howe and I were caught in the milltails of running cattle. His horse was jammed tight on my left side, but on my right were running cattle. A sharp horn tip hooked into my slicker and ripped it like tearing paper. I struck out with my quirt until the steer swung away, to be hooked in the rump by another steer crowding behind.

I cut a look at Howe in a lightning flash. His lips were

skinned back and he was swinging his wet saddle slicker. We were surrounded now on all sides by running cattle.

There was a deafening crash of thunder. A rapid succession of white fireballs exploded into nothing as the next ball burst. A metallic taste filled my mouth. The tip of my tongue tingled as though I had licked a live electric wire.

Howe's shout sounded through the echoing thunder.

"We made 'er! We're out from under!"

The cattle were still on the run, though we were no longer surrounded. Possum stood tracked in the gumbo lake beside Howe's horse, the water to our stirrups. Howe's ripped slicker was gripped in his hand. He had lost his hat and his hair was plastered down on his skull. His shirt was ripped and torn. His eyes were bloodshot slivers.

In the sheet lightning we could see the slow milling cattle that made a huge dark blot a quarter mile away. Cowpunchers sloshed their tired horses through the muddy water as they rode around the played out herd.

"We must be a good five miles from camp," Howe said looking at his watch. "Four o'clock in the mornin'." His grin was twisted.

Brewster rode up, humped over the saddle horn, shivering. His slicker hung in shreds and his face was gray with fatigue. He had aged ten years. His eyes, squinted and bloodshot, looked me over, then he managed a faint grin. "Thank God you're all right, boy," he said, and he meant every word of it.

"The lightnin' struck in the broad middle, splittin' the herd and killin' about thirty head of cattle," Brewster

161

talked through chattering teeth. "Wash Lampkin got hit. His horse got killed but he's still breathing."

Brewster sent some of the men out to locate Jack Davis and the remuda. When the horses came in, he told Howe to see that the nighthawk fetched the bed wagon over to where Wash was stretched out on a saddle blanket. And to bring Old Tex's jug and a pot of coffee, and Wash's bed.

"You better go to camp, Horace," Howe said.

"I'm stayin' on herd with Old Tex and a couple of the boys," Brewster reined his mud-spattered horse and headed back.

Howe and I rode to camp. The first gray of dawn showed and the storm had eased off when the jangle of horse bells sounded through a misty fog that had settled across the wide benchland. We could hear the nighthawk's raucous voice and his blacksnake popping.

Then the remuda appeared like some conjure trick. Humpy Jack's yellow slickered form swayed and bobbed in the saddle as he hazed the horses through muddy water. He was forking a fresh horse with its tail braided and tied up to keep it from balling in the mud. He was in a gleeful, chuckling mood when we met him a mile this side of camp.

"May the howlin' wolves never cease till they ketch the man who sold Buffalo Bill the tanglefoot!" He let out a high pitched cackle. "I picked up fifty-sixty head of strays that drifted up from Sun Prairie. If you want to see four drowned-out, sorry lookin' roundup outfits, ride over to the edge and look down yonder. There ain't a nighthawk down there with enough horses to mount his outfit, and those four big day herds are mixed and scattered from hell to breakfast."

Humpy Jack's blacksnake popped like a pistol. His lean face, with its hawk-beaked nose, was pinched with cold. The week's growth of wiry red whiskers stood out like hog bristles. His eyes were bloodshot slivers.

"Wash Lampkin's horse was killed by lightnin'," Howe told the nighthawk. "Wash is out like Nellie's eye but still alive. Brewster wants you to haul the bed wagon over to where he is."

The grin died on the nighthawk's face. I knew that he and Wash Lampkin were good friends.

Humpy Jack lost no time hazing the remuda inside the rope corral. He barked orders to empty the bed wagon. Sets of chain harness were dug out of the muck and a four-horse team harnessed. Wash's bed was spread on the floor of the wagon. George L. fastened down a big pot of steaming black coffee. I put in the jug.

Humpy Jack drove off in a spray of muddy water. Howe, on a fresh horse, rode ahead to pilot the wagon. Most of the cowpunchers had come to camp. All of us saddled fresh horses, scraping the sticky gumbo from the tails and plaiting them, and tying them above the hocks.

George L. had hot grub and coffee on the stove. For once the cranky roundup cook never complained as the cowpunchers tracked mud in the mess tent.

We piled our plates with food and filled coffee cups and carried them inside the warm bed tent. The fire was hot in the sheet-iron stove and I backed up against it and ate standing up in my wet clothes. Steam came from my curly haired chaps, and as I warned up inside they gave off a fetid rank stench.

"Somethin' dead in here," a cowpuncher lifted the tent flap to let in some fresh air.

"Stinks worse than a mess of skunks," another cowpuncher carried his grub outside and headed for the mess tent.

A cowpuncher standing beside me backed off, sniffing as he eyed me from hat to boots. "You been rollin' in a dead carcass, kid?" he asked.

Others started backing off, looking me over.

"It's those dog-hair chaps that's stinking up the whole tent," the cowpuncher near me said.

"Take 'em outside," someone suggested.

"If I was you," another one said, "I'd shore bury those billygoat leggin's."

"They're bearskin," I said meekly as I backed outside. "Genuine bearskin," I repeated.

Outside I kicked the chaps off and went over to the mess tent. George L. gave me a rag to wipe off my boots and some grease to rub into the damp leather to soften it before it had a chance to harden.

Old Tex, Brewster and Howe were riding alongside the bed wagon Humpy Jack drove. They carried Wash Lampkin into the mess tent, bed and all, and laid him down gently. His eyes were open but they had a glassy look and he seemed to be dazed.

Old Tex was shivering. He looked bent over and shriveled. His hands shook as he filled a coffee cup and warmed his cramped fingers around it.

164

We all stood around with coffee cups in our hands, the helpless way men watch another man die. But Wash wasn't dying. He was able to swallow some whisky and the glazed look gradually left his eyes. He moved his head slowly from side to side and muttered weakly that his skull felt like a red-hot tangle of barbwire.

Old Tex and Brewster stripped and put on dry clothes. After they ate, Old Tex went back to the day herd.

Tom McDonald, the Bear Pool wagon boss, and three cow hands from the other outfits rode up.

"Every outfit on Sun Prairie's afoot and bogged down," he said as he splashed coffee into a tin cup. "We're out huntin' horses."

Humpy Jack's whiskered face spread in a grin. He said he'd picked up enough stray horses during his night's travels to mount fifty cow hands. Humpy Jack had lived up to his rep as the best nighthawk in the country, and he was in a gloating mood that morning. He told us afterwards that he'd held the remuda of horses in a fenced pasture during the storm.

Brewster told Tom McDonald to take what horses he needed and to pass the word along to the other outfits that his men would pick up any stray horses or cattle they found. It would take a couple of days for Sun Prairie to dry out enough to work the cattle. Meanwhile, Old Tex would graze the Circle C beef herd on the high benchland, while the outfits on the flat were digging out.

It wasn't in Brewster's nature to brag about anything. He said if it hadn't been for Old Tex the Circle C would be in the same fix as the others. He was taking no credit himself beyond saying his outfit got off lucky.

As we rode away from camp to the bedded herd, we could see the signs of the stampede. The trampled grass and churned up mud made a wide swath. Broken off horns were on the ground and a couple of dozen crippled steers had been shot to end their suffering, their throats cut to let the blood out.

Brewster had sent word to the half-breed camp in the Larb Hills to fetch their wagons and take away the fresh killed meat.

We spent the morning rounding up about a hundred head of our own steers that had gotten away. When we dropped them in the day herd, we rode back to camp. A raw wind had scattered the low gray overhang into scudding clouds. By noon, the sky was clean-swept and cold blue. The sun had little warmth. The lake of water had disappeared, except for the water holes. The hoofs of our horses sank fetlock deep in the clay gumbo. A fifteen mile ride made a stout horse leg weary.

Except for the men on day herd with Old Tex, there was nothing for the rest of us to do but roundside at camp.

Wash Lampkin was up and dressed. He said he felt all right, except for the red-hot needles at work in his skull. Brewster fed him some whisky and put him back to bed and told him to stay there.

When Brewster said he was going over to see how the other four outfits were making out, I asked if I could go along and he said I could, providing I could stay awake that long.

166

Somehow, I didn't feel sleepy. I wanted to find Little Joe Reynolds and tell him how I was caught in the cattle stampede. My chaps were still damp and strong smelling when I pulled them on while Brewster finished his coffee.

I remembered the cat and got a can of milk from my bed and opened it. Blackstrap had burrowed into some empty sacks in the mess wagon and gone to sleep. He came alive when I started to pour the milk into his dish. I was half sitting on the edge of the wagon seat when he let out a snarl and jumped on my chaps with all four feet clawing.

It caught me off balance and I went over backwards, landing on my back in the mud beside the front wheel, with the tomcat still clawing and spitting and snarling as he raked the fur. His yowls woke every man in camp.

I managed to scramble to my feet and Blackstrap made it back to the high wagon seat in one jump. He perched there, back arched, spitting down at me. I was mud smeared and a lot of the canned milk had spilled over me.

I saw Brewster glance at the milk can before I had a chance to tromp it into the mud. Not that it made much difference one way or another, but I felt as guilty as I looked. There was the can to show I was the sheep camp robber. The cowpunchers were all grinning at me.

All I needed was for Jack Teal to ride up about now, I told them, and they could die laughing. I was bawling mad.

"Keep on those skunk-hide leggin's," one cow hand said, "and I'll guarantee Teal will turn you loose." Others made more suggestions.

Humpy Jack shoved his head through the tepee flap and told them to lay off and let a man get some sleep.

167

"It was you gave the kid the chaps that stink like a monkey cage, Jack," one of them said. "We've been makin' bets what kind of fur they're made of. Supposin' you settle the argument."

"Those chaps are made from the hide of a sidehill gouger," Humpy Jack cackled. "The legs on his left side are twice as long as those on his right side. He can outrace a mountain goat on a steep slat, providin' he travels to the left. Head a sidehill gouger around so he travels to the right and he'll fall over.

"The curly haired sidehill gouger is a scarce animal nowadays. Well nigh extinct in this country. Teddy Roosevelt killed that man-eatin' gouger in darkest Africa and had the hide tanned by the head-hunter tribe of cannibals, over a fire of elephant chips. He made me a present of the hide when I broke some broncs for his outfit on the Little Missouri in Dakota. Those chaps have a historic value and by rights belong in a museum.

"Now supposin' you boneheads quit hollerin' and let a man get his sleep. I was in the saddle all night." Jack spoke waspishly and pulled his head in.

168

CHAPTER SIXTEEN

Little Joe Says Good-by

"Tomorrow morning," Brewster told the Circle C men while we were eating supper, "the five outfits will split up, and the last big general roundup in this part of the country will be over. There will probably never be another roundup where five big outfits work together."

The ramrod left an empty silence behind when he walked away. He saddled his night horse and rode out to where Old Tex was grazing the beef herd onto the bedground.

I was getting a cocklebur out of Possum's tail when Little Joe Reynolds rode up and swung down from his saddle.

"I rode over to say good-by," he said. "Uncle Joe is sending me back to Texas."

"How about a game of mumble-peg?" I suggested.

We squatted down beside the bed wagon and I got out my jackknife. It was one of Jackknife Ben's, who had a shop near the Union Stockyards in Chicago. Brewster had brought it back to me. It was a three-bladed knife of good steel, with the picture of a Texas longhorn on both sides of the handle. I knew that Little Joe admired it.

He had a big knife with a buckhorn handle. It had an awl blade in addition to the three regular blades, and a corkscrew that folded down along the back. It was sort of

169

clumsy and too heavy and a little off-balance for playing mumble-peg, but he was too full of pride to borrow mine. That was the main reason I always beat him and he'd have to pull the peg from the ground with his teeth.

I knew that Little Joe hated to say good-by as much as I did. We were good friends and had been in a couple of tight places together. Our arguments sometimes had been hot, but we swapped grins the next time we met.

I was trying to lose this last game without letting on. But Little Joe kept fumbling and missing, until I finally caught on that he was missing on purpose to let me win.

We came to the move called "hopping the old lady across the fence" where you shoved the knife blade into the ground at a slant. Holding the left hand upward on the ground about 6 or 8 inches from the knife, you batted the knife over the other hand. The blade had to stick in the ground with enough upward slant to get two fingers under the handle.

Little Joe batted his clumsy knife almost into my lap where I sat cross-legged. It landed flat.

I held my knife by the long blade tip and flipped it between his crossed legs, the point an inch in the ground. I picked up his knife. "Let's swap knives," I tried to make my suggestion sound offhanded. "I'll throw in a snakeskin to boot," I added.

I watched his eyes shine as he picked up my knife. He looked at the picture of the Texas longhorn and grinned, and the swap was made.

I unrolled my bed and untied the whang leather string around my warsack. I had the skins of half a dozen black diamond rattlers I had killed. All of the snakes had been three feet or more in length with the rattles on. I dried the skins by sprinkling the sticky underside with salt and tacking them to boards, then I worked the stiffness out until the skins were pliable. Then I rolled the skin up, tail first, and put a wide rubber band around it.

The snakeskins had a sickening sweet smell. I came in for a lot of rough joshing and horseplay when some cowpuncher would take off his hat and fan me off. My clothes would be saturated with the snake odor and it took half a day for the wind to blow it away.

When I got to Great Falls, I would swap the skins off to the town kids and tack a couple to the wall of my room.

I gave Little Joe the pick of the snakeskins and in return he gave me a Mexican carved leather hatband he took off his hat.

Little Joe kept putting off leaving as we squatted beside the wagon, eating fresh sugar doughnuts that George L. had made.

Finally Little Joe and I shook hands awkwardly and neither of us could find anything to say. There was an aching lump in my throat as I watched him ride over the hill and out of sight.

CHAPTER SEVENTEEN

Making a Hand

There was a thin drizzle in the early gray dawn, driven by a raw wind that came down across the Canadian line, cold enough to have blown off the snow-capped Canadian Rockies.

I had on all the henskin clothes in my warsack, which wasn't too much; thin summer underwear and a sateen shirt and overalls. I had no coat under my saddle slicker. My buckskin gloves were worn paper thin.

I walked around, hunched over and shriveled inside the cold slicker that was stiff and crackling. My face felt numb and pinched and my hands stiff and cold. My feet felt like frozen lumps inside my wet boots. The weight of my wet dog-hair chaps dragged at the belt. I had to clamp my jaws to keep my teeth from chattering. My neck was pulled in turtlewise, the rain dripping from my hat brim felt like ice water down the back of my neck.

The cold empty knot inside my belly had nothing to do with the weather. This was the day Bob and Will were due to show up to trim the beef herd. My father too would be out.

Snowflake leaned his head over the rope corral and I slipped the rope over his head and led him out. This was the dread day I had been shoving back in my mind for the two weeks of carefree days and nights on the roundup.

I'd tried my best to make a hand. I had asked no favors and had gotten none. Roping the sheep and robbing the camp, and losing the remuda were the only black marks against my record.

The first question my father would ask when he drove up in his top buggy would be direct and to the point. Had I made a hand?

If Brewster told him I made good and had the makings of a cow hand, that would please him. But the ramrod's praise might not register with Bob and Will. They might figure he had babied me along, giving me the best of it.

Wallace wouldn't be here to take my part, as he always did. There was a big mountain sheep in the main range of the Rockies, and Wallace was getting his pack outfit ready when I had left on the roundup. He was after that mountain sheep before the first snow would fall.

Snowflake had rolled. I got a flat stick and was scraping the mud from his back when Brewster came up, leading a short-coupled, chunky muscled roan gelding named Dixie. Dixie was one of the best cutting horses in the remuda. He was a quarter horse and fast as greased lightning, quick as a cat.

"Turn Snowflake loose," Brewster told me. "I want you to make a showin' when Bob and Will come out to the herd. Give Dixie his head and he'll do the steer cuttin'. It'll give me a leg to stand on when they see you're makin' a hand. Maybe they'll quit bellyachin' and let up on you

173

for a change." He put a hackamore on Dixie and looped the braided horsehair rope into one rein.

The cold empty knot inside me thawed. I ran my hand along the roan's back and threw my saddle blanket on. It was a single blanket, ragged and threadbare, so I used it for a sweat blanket. On top of it I put an almost new double Navajo saddle blanket I picked up in the bed wagon. I didn't know who it belonged to but I was only borrowing it for today. It was a red and black diamond pattern on a gray background. It made my saddle sit up a little high on Dixie's withers but I sure didn't aim to rub a gall sore on his back. I tightened the cinch and let him stand.

Most horses swell up when the cinch tightens, so you let them stand a few minutes and then pull the latigo strap up a couple of inches. A tight cinched saddle was necessary for roping or cutting cattle.

I waited outside the mess tent. I pulled my hat down and faced into the wind, letting the drizzle slash at my face and squinted eyes. Then I saw my father driving Nip and Tuck. He was alone in the buggy.

His black slicker was buttoned up under his gray beard. His hat was pulled down and his gloved hands held a tight rein on the Tucker bays. He circled the wagons and rope corral once before he reined the team to a sliding halt.

Howe and Brewster came out of the mess tent to hold the team. I ground-tied Dixie who had been trained to stand with the bridle reins dropped on the ground. I was unfastening the tugs of the buggy when my father looked me over and said, "From what I hear, son, you've been

174

makin' a hand." I saw the twinkle in his eyes as he headed for the mess tent.

Howe and Brewster took care of the team.

"What do you have for breakfast, George L.?" I heard my father ask.

"Flapjacks. I hid out a can of syrup."

"Make me a little toast, George L."

"Yes, sir."

"That a fresh pot of coffee?"

"Fresh half an hour ago, Mister Coburn."

"I'll take a cup of tea, George L."

It was the same old routine. If George L. had said toast, my father would have asked for flapjacks. If he'd said he had a pot of tea brewing, it would have been coffee he wanted. It was a sort of ritual that never varied at the ranch, on the roundup or at home—one of my father's little jokes and George L. never seemed to catch on.

I was in a cold sweat to get out to the herd before Bob and Will drove up. Brewster seemed to understand and said we might as well ride out and start whittlin' on 'em. Howe said he'd wait and come out with father when he finished breakfast.

There was no circle to ride that morning. Every cow hand in the outfit was out there holding the big herd.

Brewster and I had cut half a dozen steers by the time my father and Howe rode up. We worked a couple from the middle of the herd and laned them out to the edge where the two men sat their horses. Then Horace pointed out a big steer for me to cut. I gave Dixie his head and let him do the work he loved to do. We goosed the steer when we reached the edge of the holdup and he ran out between Howe and my father. Howe hazed him halfway to the holding cut while my father sat and watched me turn Dixie back into the herd.

It was still drizzling but the wind had died down. The chill was gone and I was sweating a little inside my slicker. It was clammy sweat because I was as nervous as a cat on a hot griddle. I had sighted Bob and Will as they drove up to camp. Now they were riding toward the herd.

Brewster and I laned a steer out as they reined up. I saw Bob eye me on Dixie, and I could feel the cold look in his eyes a hundred feet away. I knew he'd be asking how come I was riding Dixie instead of Snowflake, and I had a notion Brewster would be in for a dressing down.

What Bob didn't know was that father had made Horace a present of Dixie and he no longer belonged to the Circle C.

Brewster pointed out a big brockle-faced steer and said, "Work that one from the middle, then shotgun him out under their noses and make a showin'." Hard blue sparks showed in his puckered eyes.

The brockle-faced steer was ornery. He kept trying to turn and dodge back. Long ago Brewster had taught me to carry the end of my ketch-rope in my right hand, to give a rider a balance in the saddle, he said. Besides it was something to hold in your hand, to keep from grabbing the saddle horn.

I knew that every move I made was being watched with critical eyes. I could see Bob sitting with his weight in his left stirrup, tall in the saddle.

I got the steer to the edge when he doubled back. The muddy ground was slick and Dixie slipped a little. When the steer came past, I rapped him across the eyes with the doubled wet rope. He turned back, shaking his head, and the little roan cutting horse took it from there. At the edge of the herd I knew the steer was on the prod and would turn back again, so I brought the rope down across his rump. He bawled and hooked sideways and jumped out into the open. Then he caught sight of the four men on horseback and whirled back toward the herd.

The sudden unexpected move caught me off-balance. But Dixie was wide-awake and outguessing mister steer. He squatted and whirled and jumped to head off the steer, in so many split seconds. As he came back under me I lost my right stirrup. I dropped the rope and grabbed the horn to pull me back in the saddle. Then I felt the saddle slip sideways, and the next second it was under the horse's belly.

I felt a dull thud as my back hit the ground. My left boot was hung in the stirrup and Dixie was running. My grip on the horn slipped and my face and head slammed into the muddy ground. That was the last thing I remembered.

Every cowpuncher has a dread fear of being dragged to death by a horse. Before I passed out I knew what it felt like to have that fear crystallize. I knew if I came out alive I'd carry the stark memory of those brief seconds through life.

It was like fighting to come out of a bad dream. I tried to holler but no sound came. A red pinwheel was spinning inside my head. Then I came alive, retching and vomiting.

Somebody was holding my head up, then I was eased over on my back and a wet slicker was put under my head.

I saw my father's gray bearded face as he bent over me. I tried to tell him I was all right. "I just got the wind knocked out," I forced the words out. I tried to sit up but I was being held down. I heard Brewster tell me to take it easy.

"Dixie?" I asked. "Is Dixie crippled?"

"Dixie's all right," he assured me. I tried to get up again, telling them there was nothing the matter with me. I'd got my wind knocked out, was all.

"Maybe he's right," I heard Will say. "Let him sit up, but go easy. He might be hurt inside, he was pukin' some blood."

I felt a little dizzy in a sitting position. My father held a leather covered flask to my mouth and made me take a swallow of raw whisky. I could feel it burn as it went down.

When I took a breath, pain knifed my ribs. I moved my legs and arms to see if I had any broken bones. I was too numb from shock to feel the aches and pains that would come later. I was covered with muck.

I looked up and saw Bob standing there in his shirt sleeves and I knew then that it was his slicker under my head. I told him it was all my fault for not cinching my saddle tight. I tried to force a grin but my face felt stiff.

I wanted to act game about it so I started to get to my feet. Howe and Brewster had to help me up and I stood tracked until the dizzy feeling left. Then I saw what was left of my slicker and chaps, both torn to shreds. One leg of the dog-hair chaps was gone and what was left of my saddle lay in the mud, both stirrups torn off. Dixie had kicked it to pieces until the cinch broke and he was free.

I could see Dixie standing off a way, the hackamore reins hooked over the saddle horn of Brewster's horse. The little roan cutting horse was still nervous and trembling from the ordeal.

I told Brewster if he would give me a leg up I'd ride Dixie bareback to camp.

"Let the kid play out his string," I heard Bob say gruffly.

Howe gave me a leg up and rode back to camp with me. Before we got to the wagon the aches and pains started. I was lightheaded and a little tipsy from the whisky. Dixie shuffled along at a running walk, his head down like he felt ashamed. I hung on to a fistful of mane till we got to camp.

Humpy Jack and George L. helped me skin out of my muddy rags and I stood near the stove while they rubbed me down with towels. My face looked as though it had been sandpapered. The skin was peeled off my short nose. Both eyes were swollen and puffed and turning a greenish blue. When I got the sand and gravel washed off and the clotted blood from my nose, Humpy Jack smeared my face with carbolic salve.

My father had come into the mess tent as Howe up-ended my warsack on George L.'s bed. I watched my snake-skins drop out, then the Garcia saddle catalog and an order blank I had filled in. I had one clean shirt, a suit of underwear, a last pair of socks, and a pair of faded but clean Levi's.

My father had a strong dislike for the stinking snake-skins. I saw him shove them aside as he shook out my shirt

179

and handed my clothes to me. He told me he was taking me to town to have Doc Clay look me over before I caught the night train to Great Falls.

Howe was telling Humpy Jack about the accident, his voice a harsh whisper. . . . ". . . it looked like he was a goner . . . tore one leg off those chaps you gave him and there wasn't enough left of his slicker to flag a handcar . . . all a man could see was the kid in a tangle of slicker and chaps hung in the stirrup and draggin' under the horse's belly and Dixie kickin' him and the saddle loose. . . . I saw Bob with a gun in his hand just as Brewster grabbed the roan's hackamore and the kid's foot came loose. . . . I hope I never see anything like it again. . . ." Howe stopped short like he'd bit into his tongue.

I got a quick look at the little hunchback's face. It was pale and his sage green eyes were glassy. Howe, in telling the story, had forgotten that was how Jack Davis had gotten crippled for life when he was about fifteen years old.

Humpy Jack's hand shook as he went over to the stove and poured himself a cup of coffee. Then the color came back into his face and there was a harsh rattle in his chuckle when he said to me, "Them finicky nosed cowpunchers won't be bothered no more with the stink of your wet dog-hair chaps." He tried to pass it off as he carried his coffee outside.

I stood close to the stove and started shivering. I set my jaws to keep my teeth from chattering. I wasn't exactly cold, with the heat of the stove pouring on me. It was the yellow cowardice inside me that was showing. I wanted to crawl off somewhere alone so they couldn't see that I was scared, so I ducked under the canvas fly and went out into the cold drizzle.

Blackstrap was under the mess wagon, slapping at a dead rat. I squatted and rubbed behind his ragged ears. I hoped he'd still be around when I came back next summer.

Humpy Jack had put on a slicker and was walking slowly around the little roan quarter horse tied to the wagon wheel. I went over and rubbed the small furry ears, and Dixie rubbed his head on the old mackinaw I had on that came below my knees.

The strange part of it was I no longer had the shakes. When I realized it, I made some kind of a noise that passed for a laugh. Humpy Jack understood what the sound meant. He gripped my shoulder and said, "It'll come back at times, creep up on you while you're asleep, and you'll live it over and over and come awake scared. It took guts for you to ride Dixie to camp, but that was the medicine you needed."

I told the nighthawk it wasn't that, exactly. I had to show them all I wasn't afraid to ride Dixie. I was more scared of them than I was of the horse.

Jack said it amounted to the same thing and that doubled the odds. He unbraided Dixie's tail while he was talking and I kept rubbing behind his ears. The little roan kept muzzling me as if to tell me he was ashamed and sorry for getting spooked.

My father drove up in his buggy and I climbed in. George L. put in my war sack. I pulled the Navajo lap robe up across my legs. The Tucker bays reared back on their hind legs, front feet pawing the air, before we got going.

I held on with both hands as the buggy bounced over clumps of sagebrush. The wind whipped my father's gray beard as he sawed on the lines and pulled the team down to a long trot. His blue eyes were bright as he talked to the horses.

I saw Snowflake grazing with a couple of his cronies, rump to the wind. That fat white pony was always eating. He looked up as the buggy passed and I leaned out to get a last farewell look at him. I hoped he'd winter in good shape. But I knew he'd take care of himself, as he always did.

CHAPTER EIGHTEEN

I Leave the Roundup

That buggy ride from the roundup camp to Malta seemed a year long. I hunched under the lap robe and shivered and shook and toughed it out the best I knew how.

Everytime we hit a chuck hole it sent pains like dull knives through me from head to foot. My jaws ached from gritting my teeth to keep from yelping. Even my eyeballs ached in their bruised sockets. I was beat up and bone cold and sick from disappointment, about as miserable a human as ever lived to tell the tale.

But there was no average in feeling sorry for myself. Nobody feels sorry for a quitter, so I'd play my string out. It could be a lot worse. Anyhow, I hadn't crippled the roan cutting horse, and I had outgrown the saddle that lay scattered back yonder in the mud where Dixie had kicked it loose.

My father kept asking me how I felt. Did I hurt much? Where did it hurt the most?

"It hurts all over," I told him, "but spread out that way it isn't too bad. If I had a saddle I could go on day herd this afternoon," I added hopefully. "I could make a hand at the shipping yards, too. Snowflake rides easy as a rocking chair."

His bearded lips smiled faintly as he looked sideways at

me. "The Circle C outfit will just have to worry along short-handed," he said.

We pulled up in front of the Great Northern Hotel. It was a gray day, filled with cold drizzling rain. The streets looked deserted. This was the day the Circle Diamond were shipping and there wasn't a cowpuncher in town.

"I'll have to put up the team," father said. "Think you can make it up to my room alone?" he asked worriedly.

"Yes, sir." I tried not to limp as I crossed the plank sidewalk and shoved open the door.

"I'll stop at Doc Clay's office and send him over," he called to me. "Get into a hot tub."

A few minutes later Doc Clay came in and had me soaking in a hot tub, sponging me off with medicated liquid soap. He was drying me off in the bathroom when my father came in.

"How bad is the boy hurt, Doc?" his voice sounded anxious. He was looking me over where I stood naked as a jay bird. "He looks like he tangled with a grizzly."

"It looks worse than it is," Doc Clay said, helping me to the edge of the bed where he made me sit up straight.

He gave me a couple of little white pills before he helped me undress and the worst of the pain was gone. I was feeling drowsy.

After a quick examination, Doc said, "Cracked collarbone and a few ribs that need taping up."

He set the fractured collarbone and taped it with whalebone splints. Then he fastened strip after strip of adhesive tape across my cracked ribs.

It hurt. I didn't dare take a deep breath on account of

the stablike pains through my chest. I tried to grin while my father held me steady.

"The boy's lucky to be alive," he said, telling Doc Clay what had happened. "It's something a man can't forget, Doc. I'm still a little shaky. The boy's got what it takes, never let out a whimper. If he had his way he'd still be on the roundup, tryin' to make a hand."

"Game as a pit bull pup," I heard Doc's faraway voice as he helped me into bed. I was kind of dizzy and glad to lie back. I shut my eyes and passed out like a candle blown by a black wind.

I came awake hours later with the gas light from the wall bracket shining in my eyes. Frank Howe was asleep in the armchair beside the bed. He awoke when he heard me move. He was dressed to the nines in a new blue serge suit and wearing his town boots. He had gotten the works at Shorty's Barber Shop and smelled of bay rum and talcum powder and bar whisky.

My mouth felt like it was stuffed with dry cotton. Howe filled a tumbler with ice water from a pitcher and held my head propped up while I drank.

The glass was almost empty when I saw it. A brand-new, hand-tooled, round-skirted saddle that was straddle of the wooden footboard of the bed. I choked on a mouthful of water and sprayed the blanket.

"You were dead to the world," Howe chuckled as he placed a second pillow behind my back so I could sit up straight, "when Bob fetched it in."

"Bob?" I thought he had gotten it wrong.

"Your brother Bob, the one you've been cussin' out in your sleep."

If this was one of Howe's jokes I wasn't going to get caught in the trap so I let it ride.

Howe said, "Bob ordered the hull made on a small-sized tree from the Garcia Saddle Company at Elko, Nevada."

"When was that?" My voice had a tight, dry sound.

"A week or two after the train holdup on July Third. He said you'd outgrown your saddle and I helped him pick this one out."

It was as if somebody had filled my eyes with alkali dust. I didn't dare trust my voice.

"The saddle's been at the depot for ten days without anybody knowin' it. Bob found it in the baggage room when he checked his trunk this afternoon. He lugged it over and unsacked it and saddled the bed board. He had to catch the train for Chicago. Said to tell you to tighten your cinch the next time you ride a cuttin' horse into a herd of cattle. Then he left me here to ride herd on you."

There was a new split-ear headstall, with a long shanked silver mounted bit. My initials were engraved on the silver conchos. There was a pair of silver mounted spurs, and a new Navajo saddle blanket under the saddle. Exactly what I had filled in on the order blank that was in my warsack.

I swallowed a couple of times before I asked, "The rest of the outfit?"

Howe chuckled. "I copied what you'd put down on that order blank in your warsack and passed the hat around camp one day when you weren't there. The stuff came a few days ago and Bob brought it to town from the ranch this morning. Will ordered you a pair of Angora chaps that should be here any day. Will's gone to Chicago with John Survant and his trainload of Circle Diamond beef. Before he left, he said to tell you he was making you a present of Eclipse."

Eclipse was a light sorrel gelding covered with white spots the size of a dollar, all over his hide—a freak marked Apaloosa, built like a quarter horse, about the same size as Dixie, and one of the top cutting horses in the Circle C remuda. Will had trained the horse himself and he could remove the bridle and Eclipse would cut the rankest steer out of the herd.

Will had often been kidded about what they called his "Injun" pony, but I knew it took more than a lot of joshing to get him to part with Eclipse. He had refused big money for that spotted cutting horse. If he was really giving me Eclipse, it was one for the book.

I kept swallowing the hard lump in my throat and batting my eyes. I managed to say, "Bob and Will have sure treated me fine."

"Yeah," Howe said. "They told Brewster and the rest of us that you had plenty guts. What it takes to make a cow hand."

He said my father had gone to Chicago on the same train with Bob. They'd meet Will there and attend a big cattlemen's convention.

I slid out of bed. I had on one of my father's short-tailed nightshirts and I must have looked comical. But I just had to get to that saddle. In spite of the pain that was still with me I managed to straddle it.

The hand-tooled leather was truly a work of art. When I rubbed my hand across the round saddle skirts I could feel the deeply carved rose pattern, which only the skilled workmanship of the Mexican leather carvers in the Garcia saddle shop could turn out. The bucking roll of quilted buckskin across the fork of the saddle made it a perfect fit. It was a thirteen-inch tree, near as I could figure, with a little swell to the fork.

It was a young cowboy's dream come true. The bridle and bit and spurs were frosting on the cake. With that outfit on the spotted cutting horse Eclipse, I would have plenty of reason to admire my shadow as I rode along. And I had something to look forward to for next summer's vacation.

Brewster came in while I was admiring my saddle. He had my valise with him. "Hard lines, pardner," he said. "You're on your way back to school."

"This makes up for missing the shipping," I said. "Did you get bawled out on account of what happened?"

"I beat 'em to it," Brewster grinned. "Told 'em it was them sittin' their horses that spooked the steer back. I'll see to it that you get a good cuttin' horse in your string."

"I have Snowflake and Moss Agate, and now Will's given me Eclipse," I said.

"I know. Will told me. Those two, with Possum for a night horse, and a few more, you'll be fixed with a top string." Brewster gave Frank Howe a hard look, then said, "You're dressed like you're goin' places, Howe. Don't you know we're movin' the beef herd off the bedground at three in the morning. The cars are ready for shipping."

"The Old Gent said I was to ride herd on this shirttail

188

outlaw till he got to Great Falls. Doc Clay says he's in no shape to travel alone." Howe's grin spread. "Besides, I got important business to tend to in Great Falls. It might be a week before I get back."

"The last time you overdrew your pay two months in advance, you claimed you were gettin' married. You showed up broke and still single, a week later. What's the big reason this time?"

"Charlie Russell is paintin' a picture of me and Joe Reynolds ropin' the grizzly bear in the Larb Hills last spring on the calf roundup. He wants me to sit a horse while he sketches. I'm bringin' Charlie back with me so he can draw Joe and me together. We'll take a pack outfit to the exact spot we roped that bear in the Larb Hills."

"Pick up the marbles, Howe," Brewster said resignedly.

They helped me dress. I was handicapped with my arm in a sling. I wore my black sateen shirt and Levi's and a new Stetson hat that Howe had bought for me at the Mercantile. I left my town clothes in my valise. My mother wasn't here to make me put them on.

By the time they sacked my saddle and outfit, we had only about twenty minutes until traintime. Howe said we'd eat supper in the dining car, which pleased me.

The hotel porter took our luggage to the depot in a pushcart and I walked over with Brewster and Howe.

The same Negro porter was there with his stool, and Nig Edwards swung down the steps, his conductor's cap at a slant on his iron gray hair. When he hollered "All Aboard" I shook hands with Brewster and said good-by until next summer vacation.

189

Howe and I had a section to ourselves. When the train pulled out we went back to the observation car and sat on the canvas stools on the rear platform. We had to watch out not to get cinders in our eyes.

When we came to the Milk River bridge near Wagner, Howe showed me where the Wild Bunch had held up the train last July. He pointed out the spot where the sheepherder had sat his horse while the holdup was going on, until Kid Curry had dropped a couple of shots his way and the shepherd had lost his curiosity and made himself scarce. Howe had every detail down pat like he had been there. But he claimed he was fifty miles away that day.

Howe took the upper berth and let me have the lower, so that I could look out the window, which I did far into the night. This was my cow country and I was a part of it. I felt sad and lonesome about leaving it as I stared out across the moonlit prairie at some distant ranch.

Tomorrow I would be in Great Falls, riding a bike instead of a cow pony. I would be back in school and with my own gang again. And for the first time I realized how lonesome for them I actually was.

Next Saturday we would all gather and ride our bikes to the sand hills. We would build a campfire after dark and while we sat around it I would sing the songs Frank Howe had sung on the roundup as we rode around the bedded herd, and I would tell the gang all about my first roundup and how lucky I was to be alive. It was something to look forward to.